Aviation Elite Units

MW01009319

# No 43 'Fighting Cocks' Squadron

Aviation Elite Units • 9

OSPREY
PUBLISHING

# No 43 'Fighting Cocks' Squadron

Andy Saunders

Series editor  Tony Holmes

**Front cover**
On 5 September 1940 Sgt Alex Hurry took off from Tangmere on No 43 Sqn's second scramble of the day in Hurricane P3386 FT-E. His mount on this day had recently become the most successful aircraft on the squadron, having destroyed 12 enemy aircraft in the hands of four different pilots. During this particular engagement, Alex Hurry intercepted and shot down a Bf 109, whose destruction was confirmed. His Combat Report for this action was very specific, clearly identifying the location of the crash, and thus the identity of the aeroplane and its pilot. His Combat Report reads as follows;

'I was flying in Blue section as Blue 3 at 20,000 ft over Biggin Hill when Blue 1 turned and dived. I followed but lost him in thick haze and joined up with Blue 2 at 10,000 ft and climbed again to re-join the squadron. At 18,000 ft at 1605 hrs over Maidstone I sighted some 30-40 Me 109s heading west north-west at 15,000 ft. I climbed into the sun and gave the "Tally Ho!", then turned and dived on to the rear vic of five enemy aircraft. During my dive they turned south and I carried out a quarter attack on the outer enemy aircraft. The length of my burst was five seconds. The enemy aircraft half rolled and dived and I followed as the remaining four aircraft were turning to attack me. The enemy aircraft pulled out at 5000 ft and flew south. I caught him again 12 miles north-west of Dungeness and fired a burst of six seconds. He caught fire, half rolled and dived vertically into the ground near Appledore Station, about ten miles north-west of Dungeness. No attempt made at evasion. Enemy markings were dull green with white wingtips and silver (sic) undersurfaces. I did not see the pilot bale out. The weather was hazy with 4/10ths cloud at 17,000 ft. Visibility 12 miles.'

Hurry's victim was Bf 109E-1 Wk-Nr 3627 of 5./JG 27, flown by Oberleutnant Helmut Strobl, who was initially posted missing in action by the Luftwaffe. The Messerschmitt, along with the remains of Strobl, were found close to Appledore Station exactly 46 years later on 5 September 1986
(*Cover artwork by Iain Wyllie*)

**Dedication**
**For my eldest son. Jonathan.**

First published in Great Britain in 2003 by Osprey Publishing
Elms Court, Chapel Way, Botley, Oxford, OX2 9LP

ISBN 1 84176 439 6

Edited by Tony Holmes
Page design by Mark Holt
Cover Artwork by Iain Wyllie
Aircraft Profiles by Chris Davey
Origination by Grasmere Digital Imaging, Leeds, UK
Printed in China through Bookbuilders Hong Kong

03 04 05 06 07    10 9 8 7 6 5 4 3 2 1

ACKNOWLEDGEMENTS
I would like to thank Peter Arnold, Peter Cornwell, Paul Cole, Issie Diss, the Rt Hon Ian Duncan-Smith MP, Norman Franks, Roger Freeman, Chris Goss, Celia Gregory, John Hewitt, Stephen Hill, Ian Hutton, Bruce Robertson, Andy Thomas and the No 43 Sqn Association for the provision of photographs included within this volume.

EDITORS NOTE
To make this new series as authoritative as possible, the Editor would be interested in hearing from any individual who may have relevant photographs, documentation or first-hand experiences relating to the world's elite combat units, their pilots and aircraft, of the various theatres of war. Any material used will be credited to its original source. Please write to Tony Holmes at 10 Prospect Road, Sevenoaks, Kent, TN13 3UA, Great Britain, or by e-mail at: tony.holmes@osprey-jets.freeserve.co.uk

# CONTENTS

# INTRODUCTION

**M**y interest in the exploits of No 43 Sqn date back to the late 1960s and early 1970s when I began to research enemy losses over my home county of Sussex during the Battle of Britain. Very soon it became clear to me that time and again the demise of Luftwaffe aeroplanes in the county could be attributed to one particular squadron. Of course, that squadron was No 43.

Given that the unit was based for much of 1940 at RAF Tangmere in Sussex it is, perhaps, less than surprising that the 'Fighting Cocks' should have been involved in many of these victories. Sadly, though, many of the losses were not all one sided, and a significant number of No 43 Sqn pilots failed to return home to Tangmere. These casualties inspired me in the early 1980s to formulate plans for the establishment of a museum at former RAF Tangmere along with my friend and colleague the late James Beedle. Jimmy became co-founder, with me, of the now thriving Tangmere Aviation Museum which opened in 1982.

In the period leading up to the museum's opening, I was privileged to become firm friends with the late Jimmy Beedle, himself a former No 43 Sqn member. Through him I was able to meet many of the then surviving No 43 Sqn members, and he also fuelled my interest in the unit, most particularly through his excellent squadron history *No 43(F) Squadron – The Fighting Cocks*. Needless to say, my interest in the unit grew along with my collection of related material.

In some small and modest way I hope that this book can reflect credit upon arguably one of the most famous squadrons in the history of RAF Fighter Command, and a squadron which still exists today in the forefront of the UK's air defence. The traditions and excellence of 'The Fighting Cocks' remain proudly upheld. Of its fliers who have failed to return through the unit's 86-year history, the squadron motto must be their epitaph – 'Gloria Finis', Glory Is The End.

Andy Saunders
Hastings, Sussex
September 2002

# LULL BEFORE THE STORM

No 43 Sqn was originally formed at Stirling on 15 April 1916 as a component squadron in the Royal Flying Corps, and it later served with some distinction on the Western Front. But, although an illustrious period in the squadron's history, it is not one that this publication seeks to cover. It is, however, important to appreciate the fine traditions of this unit which, established during World War 1, continued and were strengthened during the inter-war period.

Early days. This immaculate line up of gleaming No 43 Sqn Furies at Tangmere was photographed in 1931. Within ten years the squadron would be fighting a bloody war from this same airfield

This aerial view of RAF Tangmere depicts it in its pristine inter-war period. This is how the station looked during No 43 Sqn's spell with the Fury, and much how it was at the start of the war. The buildings, however, had by then been camouflaged, and additional runways had been built. Some of the Belfast hangars and other buildings were lost in the 16 August 1940 bombing, or subsequently during the war

A formation of No 43 Sqn Furies cruise over the Sussex countryside in the late 1930s. These aircraft were painted silver overall with bright polished cowlings, wheel discs bearing the flight colours and black and white checks on the fuselage sides and upper wings. The chequerboard markings varied in their application in that some were just black squares, with the 'white' segments left silver, and others were actually painted both black and white. During this period whisky distillers Black & White used a No 43 Sqn Fury as part of its advertising campaign, exploiting the unit's black and white checks

Although disbanded in 1919, No 43 Sqn was re-formed at Henlow in 1925, and very soon thereafter moved to RAF Tangmere on the Sussex coast – a place which the squadron later came to consider as its 'ancestral home'. Through the 1920s and 30s, the unit was equipped with Gamecocks, Siskins, Furies and, from November 1938, the Hurricane I. Whilst led by Sqn Ldr A F Brooke (1925-28) from Henlow, the unit received an Air Ministry instruction that all squadrons should seek their own badge and mottos. Brooke's solution was simple. His family motto was 'Gloria Finis', literally 'Glory Is The End'. The fact that the unit was flying Gamecocks made the badge selection simple – it would be a fighting gamecock. The rest, as they say, is history, and No 43 Sqn has ever since been known as 'The Fighting Cocks'. Quite how or why the black and white chequerboard markings came to be adopted is, though, shrouded in some mystery.

In 1938, as war clouds gathered, the bright silver Hawker Furies with their black and white check bands and fighting cock emblems were camouflaged dark earth and dark green, but with black and white undersurfaces. Not black and white checks, maybe, but as the CO, Sqn Ldr 'Dickie' Bain, pointed out 'at least still black and white!' However, the halcyon days of RAF life at Tangmere were all but over, as the once sparkling white hangars and buildings were painted in drab greens and browns and air raid shelters were constructed in

They also served! LAC 'Pompey' Edwards gives the thumbs up from astride the bonnet of a No 43 Sqn Morris-Commercial refuelling bowser at Tangmere during 1939. Men like these, the groundcrews or simply 'erks', formed an extraordinary bond with their pilots, who had to place complete trust in those who looked after the machines they took into battle. They felt a part of the squadron 'family' as much as the pilots did

Fairey Battle K7693, fitted with dual controls, served with No 43 Sqn for night flying training from February through to November 1939. It was as unloved by the Hurricane pilots as it was by those who had to fly it in combat as a bomber. Despite the training, it did nothing to help save the life of Flg Off Rotherham, who died in a Hurricane night flying accident on 22 April 1939. Delivered to the RAF in April 1938, K7693 had previously served with Nos 226 and 35 Sqns in the bomber role prior to being issued to No 43 Sqn. It was then passed on to No 20 Maintenance Unit in November 1939, before being relegated to the status of a non-flying instructional airframe in February 1940. K7693 was struck off charge in June 1942

Both of these shots were taken during the final Fury formation flight flown by No 43 Sqn for the benefit of *Aeroplane* photographer John Yoxall on 2 February 1939. The aircraft have been camouflaged overall in dark green and dark earth, with black and white undersides. Note that the squadron's 'Fighting Cock' emblem has been meticulously reapplied to the fins of all bar three of the Furies (*Aeroplane*)

abundance. Now, just about everything was drab – including the outlook on a peaceful resolution to the Munich Crisis.

Even so, although Tangmere and its aeroplanes were now daubed in warpaint, ready for war, the simple fact of the matter was that had war come, the now outdated Furies would have stood little chance. The next generation of fighters, however, were just around the corner – the Hawker Hurricane. At the end of November 1938, the first of No 43 Sqn's Hurricanes were delivered, and on 2 February 1939 a final formation of Furies was flown for the benefit of *Flight* photographer John Yoxall.

During the latter 'Fury years' there had been a progression of new pilots joining the squadron whose names would become synonymous with the history of RAF Fighter Command and, in particular, with the 'Fighting Cocks'. Amongst those names were Hallowes, Townsend, Carey, Kilmartin, Simpson, Cox, Hull and Berry. Of these, most appear in the subsequent pages of this volume.

Despite the fact that the Fury was now an outdated and outmoded fighter, it had still served to teach well the basics of air fighting to the pilots who would form the backbone of the UK's air defence once war came. That said, many of those tactics and procedures were ultimately found to be wanting once combat commenced, but that did not alter the fact that RAF fighter pilots of the period still had to follow the accepted wisdom of air fighting tactics. Practice battle climbs, air firing and formation flying were all routinely undertaken with the Furies during this period and,

Once back on the ground, John Yoxall took this classic pose of the now redundant Furies and their pilots. Included in the line up are a number of famous Battle of France and Battle of Britain pilots, including several who would make their mark on No 43 Sqn. Left to right, they are Hallowes, Christie, Carey, Kilmartin, Rotherham, Hull, Megh, Sullivan, Carswell, Bain (CO), Rosier, Simpson, Folkes, Cox and Berry (*Aeroplane*)

**Above**
One of the first Hurricane Is delivered to No 43 Sqn was L1944 FT-A (seen here with Caesar Hull). It was in this aeroplane that Flg Off Edmonds claimed a half share in a He 111 on 3 February 1940. The aircraft survived until 29 July 1940, when it crashed near Hawkinge due to engine failure, killing its pilot, Plt Off K C Campbell

**Right**
Photographed on 1 September 1939, Hurricane L1849 FT-E is hastily sandbagged at Tangmere. This aeroplane joined the squadron on 3 March 1939 and was subsequently used by Sgt Peter Ottewill to claim a He 111 off Acklington on 3 February 1940. L1849 was eventually destroyed when Plt Off John Cruttenden abandoned it near Bognor Regis after combat on 7 July 1940. The FT codes seen in this shot were newly applied, having only just replaced the pre-war NQ codes. NQ was later re-allocated to No 24 Sqn

**Right**
War Games at Tangmere in July 1939. A gas-caped and gas-masked fitter on No 43 Sqn poses with one of the squadron's early NQ-coded Hurricanes. Groundcrews practised refuelling, re-arming and servicing Hurricanes in this cumbersome kit during these pre-war exercises. Thankfully, when the war finally came the need for such equipment did not materialise. This aircraft is thought to be L1744 in which Flt Lt Caesar Hull carried out the unit's first engagement on 29 January 1940. It was lost on 9 February 1940 when New Zealander Flg Off M K Carswell ditched in the North Sea

indeed, carried over in exactly the same manner to the Hurricanes, the only difference being that it was now all done that much faster!

During the Hurricane's early days with the squadron, the aircraft wore the usual day fighter scheme of the period with no other markings, although a handful of machines appear to have had the last two digits of their serial repeated in small figures on the fin – e.g. L1734 boasted a small 34 on each side of its fin. Later, the unit applied the two-letter code NQ to its aircraft, although this was subsequently changed to FT. The latter combination would be carried by the squadron throughout the entire war.

Inevitably, there would be accidents as No 43 Sqn familiarised itself on type whilst simultaneously preparing for war. Night flying, now required of the Hurricane pilots, took its toll, and on 22 April 1939 Flg Off John Rotherham was killed in an accident in L1738. Perhaps partly as a result of this accident, all pilots were required to fly dual-controlled Fairey Battle K7693 for night flying training. The dreaded Battle remained on the squadron strength from January to November 1939.

On 5 August came mobilisation, followed shortly thereafter by the United Kingdom Air Exercises – including the practice interception by No 43 Sqn of French Air Force bombers. Other practice flights were flown for the benefit of the Observer Corps, anti-aircraft co-operation and searchlight co-operation. However, from 24 August, there was comparatively little flying undertaken as No 43 Sqn battened down the hatches and prepared for the reality of war by dispersing its Hurricanes out of the vulnerable hangars and scattering them around the airfield perimeter. It would not be a long wait.

Flg Off C A 'John' Rotherham became the squadron's first fatality on Hurricanes when he was killed in a night flying accident at Tangmere in L1738 on 22 April 1939. He is pictured here shortly before his death with his puppy 'Fury'. Rotherham also appeared in the No 43 Sqn group photograph taken following the final Fury formation flight (see page 11)

Hurricane L1732 FT-E was issued to No 43 Sqn on 6 December 1938 and damaged in the hands of Flt Lt Caesar Hull on 29 August 1939 when he hit an airfield obstruction at Tangmere. The Hurricane went to the Morris Works at Cowley for repair on 18 September 1939, where this photograph was taken. From No 43 Sqn, L1732 went on to serve with Nos 7 & 6 Operational Training Units (OTU) and finally with No 286 Sqn. It was written off whilst still serving with this unit when the fighter hit high tension cables at Torcross, in Devon, and crashed on 14 May 1943. Clearly nobody in 1939 had heard of Health & Safety at work judging by the precarious jacking and trestling methods employed here! (*via Bruce Robertson*)

Hurricane L1592 (FT-C in this photograph, farthest from the camera) was issued to No 43 Sqn in early 1940, but after suffering battle damage on 1 June 1940 it was repaired and sent to No 615 Sqn where it was again damaged in combat. The aeroplane survived the war and is now a prized exhibit in the Science Museum in London

# PHONEY WAR AND FRANCE

'At any moment we expected hordes of German bombers to deliver a knock out attack on Tangmere'. So wrote the Commanding Officer of No 43 Sqn, Sqn Ldr 'Dickie' Bain, upon hearing Prime Minister Neville Chamberlain's declaration of war on 3 September 1939 – although it was to be almost one full year before the Luftwaffe brought the war directly to Tangmere. Nonetheless, the 'Fighting Cocks' did not have to wait that long for a taste of action, although they watched with envy as their rivals and neighbours at Tangmere, No 1 Sqn, packed and readied for immediate deployment to France.

Photographed on the day that war broke out, LAC Fairhead poses in front of a No 43 Sqn Hurricane I. Complete with his gas cape, the airman anxiously awaits the hordes of bombers that were expected at any moment! Note the then standard black/white undersurfaces of the Hurricane

Also photographed on 3 September 1939, an unidentified airman from No 43 Sqn takes cover in one of the many air raid shelters that were constructed at Tangmere in the months leading up to the outbreak of war. On 16 August 1940 a single member of the squadron's ground personnel, AC 1 J Young, was killed in the dive-bombing attack that devastated Tangmere

Hurricane L1737 FT-P is seen at Tangmere just days after Britain's declaration of war. The aeroplane was later crash-landed in France by Sgt Ayling on 7 June 1940 following an encounter with German fighters which all but wiped out No 43 Sqn

With World War 2 just a matter of days old, nine No 43 Sqn pilots informally pose for the camera at Tangmere. Behind them is the squadron hangar, which was destroyed in the bombing of 16 August 1940. They are, from left to right, Flg Off Edmonds (killed in action on 7 June 1940) Plt Off Woods-Scawen (killed in action on 2 September 1940), Plt Off Kilmartin, Flt Lt Hull (killed in action on 7 September 1940), Plt Off Carswell, Flt Lt Pennington-Leigh (killed on 1 June 1943), Sgt Carey, Flg Off Wilkinson (killed in action on 7 June 1940) and Sgt Steeley (killed on 18 January 1940). The ranks given are as at the time the photograph was taken

As No 1 Sqn left for the continent on 8 September, No 43 Sqn's Plt Off 'Killy' Kilmartin took off in Hurricane L1734 and fired the unit's first shots of the war whilst bringing down a stray Portsmouth barrage balloon over Farnborough with 1200 rounds. There followed other balloon shoots against escapees from the Portsmouth barrage, most notably on 17 September when Flt Lt Peter Townsend got one over Itchenor, Canadian Flg Off J L Sullivan bagged another ten miles out to sea and Rhodesian Flg Off Caesar Hull claimed a 'flamer' over Petersfield.

The days of uncertainty which followed were interspersed with periods of readiness, practice attacks and local and formation flying, including simulated low flying ground attacks on 26 September by Flg Off Hull (L1744) Plt Off Kilmartin (L1847) and Sgt Frank Carey (L1726) against the Chain Home radar sites at Pevensey, Poling and Ventnor respectively. Not long afterwards, on 7 October, Flg Off Sullivan had the dubious honour of damaging the first Squadron Hurricane during the war as he wrecked the undercarriage of L1825 landing at night in misty conditions.

But balloon busting, night operations and practice low flying attacks paled into insignificance when compared to the promise of action across the Channel, and the men of No 43 Sqn waited for news of their friends and rivals in No 1 Sqn.

On 27 October Sqn Ldr Bain was replaced by Sqn Ldr George Lott, the latter pilot duly becoming the new 'Chief Cock', as the COs of No 43 Sqn came to be irreverently known.

News from France was not long in coming, for on 30 October word arrived that No 1 Sqn had claimed a Dornier Do 17P near Toul, and just to deepen the gloom in No 43 Sqn, a rumour circulated that the unit was soon to be posted to the 'wild backwoods' of No 13 Group. With the spurs of the 'Fighting Cocks' unblooded, there appeared little prospect of that

A fighter pilot in the RAF since 1928 (when he joined No 19 Sqn as an NCO), the highly experienced Sqn Ldr Charles George Lott took command of No 43 Sqn at Tangmere in October 1939. He led the unit through its early actions over Scotland and the north-east, then Dunkirk and France, before being shot down and blinded in one eye during combat over the English Channel on 9 July 1940. Lott was subsequently awarded the DSO and DFC, and left the RAF as an air vice marshal in 1959, having by then also been awarded a CB and CBE. This formal photograph was taken at Wick in 1940. Lott's recommendation for his award of the DSO stated:

'Since 1 June this officer has led his squadron on operational patrols over Dunkirk, Amiens and Abbeville and other parts of enemy-occupied territory. In July, as leader of a section of Hurricanes, he pressed home an attack in adverse weather conditions against six Messerschmitt Me 110s. During the combat Sqn Ldr Lott's aircraft was badly hit but despite an injury, which eventually necessitated the removal of an eye, he brought his aircraft to within three miles of base before he was compelled to abandon it. He has personally destroyed two enemy aircraft and possibly another. This officer has displayed outstanding leadership and an intense desire to engage the enemy. He was awarded a DFC in May. Sqn Ldr Lott enlisted in the RAF in 1922 as a boy entrant and remustered as an aircraft apprentice in 1924. By 1928 he had become a Sergeant Pilot, receiving his commission in 1933'

situation changing as the squadron departed for RAF Acklington, in Northumberland, on 16 November, seemingly further than ever from the enemy. The desperately cold winter of 1939-40 was heightened by the dreariness of Acklington, which was blasted by biting easterly winds from the nearby North Sea. Tangmere, with its pre war RAF station comforts and apparent proximity to the promise of action, was a whole world away, and it was with anticipation of better days that the unit welcomed in the New Year. The 'Fighting Cocks' hoped for more interesting times.

Although 1940 would not disappoint the squadron's expectations, the year began on a black note when Sgt H J Steeley (L2086) and Sgt E G P Mullinger (L1734) became the unit's first wartime fatalities on 18 January when they collided at 800 ft over Broomhill whilst returning from a convoy patrol. Firm friends, the two sergeant pilots had been carrying out practice attacks on each other when their fighters struck each other. Although flying accidents occurred even in peacetime, these first two deaths brought an air of reality to the Phoney War, and were a portent of what was to come. On a brighter note, though, the squadron was finally able to engage the enemy before the month was through.

On 29 January Flg Off Hull, New Zealander Plt Off H L North and Sgt Carey were vectored onto an 'X' plot ten miles south south-east of Hartlepool, where they found a lone He 111 and immediately executed an attack before the enemy bomber vanished into low cloud. In the exchange of fire Caesar Hull's Hurricane (L1744) took a single hit from a 7.92 mm

Hurricane L1734 was issued to No 43 Sqn in December 1938, and as this photograph shows, was originally coded NQ-G. When the squadron codes were changed to FT in 1939 it became FT-G, and on 18 January 1940 L1734 was involved in a mid-air collision with L2066 whilst being flown by Sgt Mullinger. Both he and the pilot of the second Hurricane, Sgt Steeley, were killed (*via Andy Thomas*)

round, the bullet passing through the fuselage just aft of the cockpit. It was a disappointing start to No 43 Sqn's shooting war, but the following days were to bring better results.

The following day, five miles east of Coquet Island, Hull, again in L1744 (with red doped patches marking the entry and exit points of yesterday's bullet), intercepted two more He 111s along with Sgt Carey. In his Combat Report, Flg Off Hull stated;

'I sighted two enemy aircraft flying south and apparently attacking a small fishing vessel. I attacked one six times using beam to astern passes, and my number 2 (Carey) synchronised his attacks with me. The aircraft was seen to dive into the sea and break up, the crew being rescued by one of the fishing boats. No sign of the other enemy aircraft after this combat.'

At last, three months behind their rivals in both peace and war, No 43 Sqn was now blooded, and Caesar Hull, a 26-year-old Rhodesian born South African, had opened his scoring as one of the squadron's future aces.

Action, so long denied the squadron, now came thick and fast as the Luftwaffe intensified its anti-shipping attacks in the North Sea area and the 'Fighting Cocks' were called upon to repel the German eagles.

On 2 February, much of England was snow and ice bound, and in the grip of the worst winter imaginable. Fighter Command was effectively all but out of action. Not so No 43 Sqn! That night the enterprising groundcrew had improvised a device to clear the snow and prepare an acceptable runway for operations at dawn. A door torn from one of the huts was towed up and down the landing strip by tractor as a number of squadron personnel sat on the crazily skidding and sliding door. It worked, and in the absence of any overnight snow, the squadron confidently declared itself to HQ No 13 Group as 'available' from first light.

At 0900 hrs on 3 February the snow plough door came into its own as Black, Red and Blue Sections were scrambled, kicking up mud, slush, ice and snow as they roared off. Black Section (Flt Lt Townsend, Flg Off 'Tiger' Folkes and Sgt J 'Uncle' Hallowes) was vectored south at full speed, with Red Section (led by Flg Off Hull) and Blue Section (led by Flg Off J Simpson) being vectored towards the Tyne and the Farne Islands.

Flt Sgt James Hallowes was one of No 43 Sqn's outstanding pilots and aces, having served with the unit since 1936. He was awarded the DFM for his actions over France during June 1940, and had also participated in the actions over the north-east in the early months of the year. Later, he achieved a number of victories during the Battle of Britain. His DFM citation stated;

'During June 1940 Sgt Hallowes was attacking an enemy over northern France when he himself was attacked. His engine being disabled, he proceeded to glide back to friendly territory, but was again attacked when about to abandon his aircraft by parachute. He dropped back into his seat, and as the enemy aircraft passed he delivered such an effective burst of fire as to destroy his opponent. He then made a successful parachute landing'

On 3 February 1940 this He 111 became the first enemy aircraft to fall on English soil since World War 1. Claimed by Flt Lt Peter Townsend, in company with Flg Off Folkes and Sgt Hallowes, the bomber came down at Sneaton Castle Farm, near Whitby. The aircraft was 1H+FM Wk-Nr 2323 of 4./KG 26. Of the crew, Unteroffiziere Leuschake and Meyer were killed and Unteroffizier Missy badly wounded. Feldwebel Wilms was captured unhurt, but Missy was so seriously wounded that he was repatriated to Germany in 1943

Forty minutes later, and three miles east of Whitby, Townsend called 'Tally-ho. Bandit at two o'clock!' and wheeled Blue Section round to starboard in a climbing turn after a solitary He 111. Closing fast from below, Townsend opened fire and hit the starboard engine, which immediately trailed black smoke. Next, Folkes delivered a second attack from dead astern and raked the Heinkel's fuselage and tail with strikes as Hallowes manoeuvred to head off any attempt by the German to escape into cloud. The He 111 was already finished, however, and Townsend called off the attack as the bomber turned inland to crash on Bannial Flat at Sneaton Castle Farm, thus becoming the first enemy aircraft to be brought down in England during World War 2 (No 603 Sqn had already downed a He 111 at Humbie, in Scotland, on 28 October 1939). Townsend, Folkes and Hallowes were each awarded a third of a kill.

A few minutes before Black Section had engaged, Blue Section found another He 111 attacking shipping, and Flg Offs Simpson and Edmonds had left the bomber 'well alight' as it disappeared into the mist. But the day's actions were not yet over.

Scrambled again, Red Section (Flg Offs Hull and 'Crackers' Carswell and Plt Off North) claimed yet another Heinkel as damaged at 1030 hrs, and 45 minutes later Sgts Carey and Ottewill intercepted another He 111 15 miles east of Tynemouth, which was also attacking shipping. Following simultaneous beam attacks, the Heinkel lost both engines and the crew was forced to ditch. All five crew members were seen to climb out onto the wing of the floating bomber but, in unison, they all jumped into the water as Caesar Hull arrived on the scene and swept down in an ultra-low-level beat up! The outstanding successes of the 3rd, however, were tempered slightly by events six days later.

The 9 February saw another day of anti-shipping activity by He 111s off the east coast, Blue Section (Townsend, Carswell and Hallowes) attacking two He 111s near Coquet Island. The results were inconclusive, although Townsend came under intense return fire from one of the aircraft. Hallowes attacked the Heinkel to silence its defensive fire, and saw 'bits falling off' as the crew jettisoned the bomb load.

Meanwhile, Hallowes spotted a Hurricane gliding down towards the sea (L1744), and he left the Heinkel to follow down the stricken fighter. Hitting the sea five miles off Blyth, the aircraft immediately sank, whilst its pilot, Flg Off Carswell, bobbed to the surface in his Mae West. Winter survival time in the North Sea was counted in minutes, and only a few minutes at that, but luck was with Carswell as Sgt Hallowes guided a Swedish vessel to the spot to rescue 'Crackers' from a certain and unpleasant death. Despite the loss of a Hurricane, a claim of 'damaged' was allowed for the Heinkel.

Furthermore, the squadron's Operations Record Book makes no mention of Carswell's Hurricane being lost due to enemy action, merely citing 'engine trouble' as the cause. Whether or not this engine trouble was

This close up of the tail section of the Heinkel bears witness to the shooting of Peter Townsend. The whole aircraft was riddled with 0.303-in bullet holes

Hurricane FT-E sits in winter snow at Acklington in early 1940. This aircraft is again thought to be L1849 in which Sgt Ottewill claimed a He 111 on 3 February 1940, and which was lost on 7 July 1940. This aircraft can also be seen in a photograph run on page 12. A comparison of the two views clearly shows how six months of war affected the aircraft's external appearance

induced by 7.92 mm bullets is unclear, but on this evidence it does not seem that L1744 was the first No 43 Sqn aircraft to be lost through enemy action, albeit that it had earlier been the first 'Fighting Cocks' aeroplane to take hits on 29 January. Carswell, lucky to be alive, was not to return to operational flying for some three months.

Weather permitting, the squadron continued to undertake convoy patrols, although a slight thaw towards the end of the month caused a new problem as mud was thrown up into the radiators of the Hurricanes as they taxied or took off. If this menace did not cause overheating problems after take-off, it certainly created an added and unwelcome chore for the frozen fitters as they later struggled to de-mud their charges.

Mud, however, was probably not the cause of No 43 Sqn's next notable incident when Flg Off Simpson's engine failed during a night take-off on 21 February. Bouncing off the top of a haystack, Hurricane L1729 FT-S scythed off a telegraph pole and tore into woodland, smashing down no less than 36 larch trees! Luckily, the Hurricane did not burn, and Simpson walked out with a bloodied and broken nose only to find that his close friend Caesar Hull, convinced that he was dead, had already purloined his electric razor.

Better news earlier that day had seen Sgt Carey awarded the squadron's first wartime decoration when he received a well deserved DFM for 'determination and skill'.

The next day saw the last of February's spate of victories and engagements when Blue Section (Flt Lt Townsend, Flg Off Christie and Sgt C A H Ayling), on patrol over the Farne Islands, saw contrails above them at 20,000 ft. The three Hurricanes climbed on full boost, but almost at once Christie's engine coughed and died as its temperature shot off the gauge, Acklington's mud having solidly caked the fighter's big radiator. Fortunately, he managed to get back to Acklington. Continuing the pursuit, Townsend and Ayling caught up with the enemy aircraft (again a He 111) and made two passes at it. The bomber in turn went into a near vertical dive from 10,000 ft, its engines smoking and parts breaking away as it lost height and eventually plunged headlong into the sea.

Speaking of this particular engagement post-war, Townsend told how the scene from the 1969 film *Battle of Britain* where a He 111 plunges vertically into the North Sea sent a shiver down his spine. 'That's exactly how it was' he commented.

Four days later, on the 26th, Sqn Ldr Lott led the unit to a new base further north at Wick, in Scotland, where it was charged with helping to protect the Home Fleet in Scapa Flow. Standing patrols, local flying and Convoy Patrols were again the routine, but the absence of the Heinkel shipping raiders in March – almost customary at Acklington – made the squadron wonder if the Luftwaffe was licking its wounds, and no longer willing to face the 'Fighting Cocks'. That thought, however, was dispelled on the 28th when Flg Off Hull and Sgts Ottewill, Carey and T A Gough of No 43 Sqn and Flg Off Leeson of No 605 Sqn sent a He 111 flaming into the sea eight miles off Wick.

Come April, the Luftwaffe still seemed as reluctant as ever to cross the North Sea and challenge coastal convoys in the same frequency as had previously been the case. No doubt German plans for Scandinavia and the Low Countries had kept the Luftwaffe otherwise engaged, although on the

8th a significant force of bombers headed for the Scapa area, no doubt intent on negating any threat that the Royal Navy's Home Fleet would pose to the German invasion of Norway, which had been launched earlier that day.

Nos 43, 111 and 605 Sqns (all flying Hurricanes) were scrambled to intercept, although only Green and Blue Sections of No 43 Sqn engaged the enemy. Green Section (Flg Off J D Edmonds and Sgt J Arbuthnott) found six He 111s in loose formation 40 miles east of Copinsay lighthouse and swept into a head-on attack. Splintering Perspex showered from the nose of one of the bombers and its port engine burst into flames as Edmonds arced round for a second attack. This sent the He 111 crashing into the sea, where it broke up and sank. Arbuthnott, meanwhile, singled out another of the scattering bombers and left it diving into cloud trailing white smoke.

Blue Section (Townsend and Hallowes) sighted two more Heinkels 30 miles off Duncansby Head, Townsend sending one into the sea, where it gently tipped onto its nose and slipped beneath the waves. Hallowes, meanwhile, had been recalled to base, and en route he found another pair of He 111s above the Pentland Firth, although he was only able to fire a short burst before an air line failure stopped his guns.

Leaving the enemy aircraft diving for cloud, Hallowes reluctantly landed back at Wick, only to be followed by a He 111 that bellied into the middle of the field. It turned out that this was one of the Pentland Firth aircraft at which Hallowes had fired a one second burst, unknowingly causing such damage that its pilot was unable to contemplate a return crossing of the North Sea.

These successes were tempered on 16 April by the squadron's first operational fatality. Performing a convoy patrol 40 miles east south-east of Wick, Flg Off Folkes (Green 3), flying N2550, crashed into the sea. His shocked colleagues, circling the spot, could see no trace of 'plane or pilot'. Racing to the scene, a Royal Navy destroyer could find only a patch of oil,

**He 111 1H+DP Wk-Nr 5614 of 6./KG 26 was another victim of No 43 Sqn. Intercepted by Sgt Hallowes, the Heinkel crashed on the squadron base at Wick. Oberfeldwebeln Rost and Geerdts were killed and Leutnant Weigel and Oberfeldwebel Rehbein captured**

This group shot of No 43 Sqn pilots 'at readiness' was taken in April 1940 whilst the unit was still based at a muddy Wick. These men are, from left to right, Sgt Gough, Plt Off Oelofse, Flt Lt Hull, Plt Off Woods-Scawen and Sgt Ottewill. All of them took part in the early actions over the north-east, Dunkirk and the Battle of France or the Battle of Britain. Sgt Gough was killed over Dunkirk on 1 June 1940, Plt Off Oelofse was killed south of the Isle of Wight on 8 August, Plt Off Woods-Scawen was shot down and killed near Ivychurch, in Kent, on 2 September 1940, Flt Lt Hull was shot down and killed over Purley, in Surrey, on 7 September 1940 and Sgt Ottewill was badly burned during an engagement over France on 7 June 1940. The latter pilot did not return to operational flying. Such was the toll inflicted on a typical frontline fighter squadron during World War 2

a piece of wood and a map. So died Patrick 'Tiger' Folkes, one of No 43 Sqn's pre-war Fury pilots.

By May 1940 the depletion of valued squadron pilots through postings, largely to bolster Fighter Command losses in France, was being sorely felt within No 43 Sqn. Gone were Hull, Townsend, Carey, Christie, Thom, Plenderleith, Arbuthnott and Garton, although at least some of these men would one day return to the 'Fighting Cocks'. As a finale to the Phoney War period, on the eve of the *Blitzkrieg*, Flt Lt Simpson and Sgt Ottewill engaged a Do 17 on 9 May and sent it to join No 43's brace or two of He 111s in the North Sea. Although credited with a half share of the kill, it would seem that Ottewill did not actually open fire in this engagement. The squadron tally now stood at twelve destroyed and two damaged.

As May dragged on, and all of the action was way to the south and on mainland Europe, it was inevitable that No 43 Sqn would soon move back to No 11 Group. Indeed, on 31 May, Sqn Ldr Lott led an eager squadron from Wick back to Tangmere, although his personal journey was hindered by an engine failure, forcing him to land his Hurricane (L1739) at Grangemouth, near Edinburgh, and to follow on by Miles Magister at a rather more sedate pace.

Safely at Tangmere by 1 June, No 43 Sqn considered itself back home. But this was to be no quiet homecoming with rest in the summer sun, for Operational Orders issued from HQ No 11 Group the previous day

Hurricane L1728 FT-B ended up on its nose after an accident at Wick on 13 May 1940 whilst being flown by Plt Off Oelofse. Repaired, the Hurricane eventually found its way to No 607 Sqn when the unit relieved No 43 Sqn at Tangmere in September 1940. Ultimately, this aeroplane was to carry South African Flg Off Ivor Difford of No 607 Sqn to his death following a mid-air collision with fellow No 607 Sqn pilot Plt Off A M W Scott in P3860 north of Tangmere on 7 October 1940. The latter pilot made it safely back to base

detailed Nos 43, 145 and 245 Sqns to each provide three sections as cover for the Dunkirk beaches. No 43 Sqn's contribution was Blue Section (Lott, Tony Woods-Scawen and William Wilkinson), Red Section (Simpson, Edmonds and Ottewill) and Black Section (Carswell, Hallowes and Gough). The 'Fighting Cocks' were about to discover that the Heinkel interceptions from Acklington and Wick were a mere turkey shoot. Now, they were *really* at war.

Leading the nine Hurricanes off from Tangmere at 1053 hrs, George Lott set course for Dunkirk. Later, he recalled;

'Navigation was not a problem. One just picked up the smoke plume from Dunkirk at around Brighton and followed it to North Foreland. There, you could still follow the smoke and the procession of small boats below, all strung out like lines of little ducks.'

Over Dunkirk it was every man for himself. Flung into the reality of combat, nothing could have prepared the pilots for that day.

'A' Flight No 43 Sqn at Wick again in April 1940. These pilots are, from left to right, Sgt Buck, Plt Off Woods-Scawen, Flt Lt Hull, Plt Off Wilkinson and Sgt Garton. The only pilot to live through 1940 was Geoff Garton, who was posted to No 73 Sqn in May and survived the war as an ace with seven and three shared destroyed, two probables and two damaged. Noteworthy is the cartoon emblem on the Hurricane's engine cowling immediately behind the pilots

The No 43 Sqn run-about! Most operational fighter units were allocated at least one Miles Magister as the squadron hack, or communications aircraft. At one time or another, squadron pilots would have flown it for a variety of reasons. Issued new to No 43 Sqn in July 1939 (along with P6360), P6359 was left behind at Wick for No 3 Sqn on 31 May 1940 and eventually written off by the latter unit when it crashed soon after taking off from Longman (Inverness) on 9 July 1940

Although acquitting themselves well, the sections returned without squadron new boy 21-year-old Sgt Terry Gough (Black 3), in L1758. His home at Bitterne, Hampshire, was just down the road from Tangmere, and his parents had expected him to visit that evening on his motorcycle. Sadly, no trace of him was ever found. He had become the unit's first combat casualty. Lost too was 'Crackers' Carswell on his first operational sortie since his ditching three months earlier. This time he baled out of N2584 and later returned home aboard yet another Royal Navy destroyer. Blue 2, Flg Off Tony Woods-Scawen, also had his Hurricane (L1592 FT-C) badly shot up by German fighters, although he succeeded in making it back to Tangmere. L1592 was duly repaired and reissued to No 615 Sqn, and it is now preserved in the Science Museum in London.

On the credit side, No 43 Sqn emerged from the whirling dogfights with a good bag of kills – Lott claimed a Bf 110 damaged, Edmonds a Bf 110 and a Bf 109 damaged, Ottewill two Bf 109s destroyed, Hallowes a Bf 110 and two Bf 109s destroyed, with a third *Emil* damaged, Simpson two Bf 109s destroyed and Wilkinson two Bf 109s damaged. As George Lott soberly observed, 'Poor Gough had been avenged'. Once back at Tangmere, the returning pilots found another new boy had been posted in, Flt Lt Tom Rowland joining from Gladiator II-equipped No 263 Sqn.

The next day, 2 June, was a Sunday, although it was hardly a day of rest. Indeed, No 43 Sqn was ordered off with Nos 17, 145 and 245 Sqns to patrol the Dunkirk beaches once again. This time, there were no engagements, however. The same routine was repeated on the 3rd and the 4th, although on the latter date the unit had undertaken an extraordinarily long patrol of some 2 hours and 45 minutes. Sgt J A Buck (L1824), Flt Lt Simpson (N2665), Plt Off Woods-Scawen (L1737) and Sgt Ottewill (L1608) were unable to make it all the way back to Tangmere, and landed at Shoreham Airport with barely a drop of fuel in their tanks. A shorter, but no more eventful, patrol was flown the following day.

Hurricane L1592 was badly damaged in combat whilst being flown by Plt Off Tony Woods-Scawen over Dunkirk on 1 June 1940. Repaired, it went to No 615 Sqn, with whom it served during the Battle of Britain and was again damaged. The veteran fighter is now preserved and displayed in the Science Museum in London, albeit still in the markings of No 615 Sqn. When transferred to No 43 Sqn from No 87 Sqn (L1592 had also previously served with Nos 56 and 17 Sqns), the aeroplane was fitted with a two-bladed wooden fixed-pitch Watts propeller. The Hurricane is now fitted with a variable-pitch three-bladed de Havilland propeller
(*Science Museum*)

Flt Lt Tom Rowland joined No 43 Sqn from Gladiator II-equipped No 263 Sqn as a replacement commander for 'B' Flight during early June. His first, and only, operational flight with the squadron took place on the fateful 7 June 1940 mission over France. Shot down and wounded, he did not return to operational flying with No 43 Sqn, instead later becoming a Fighter Controller

Operation *Dynamo*, the evacuation of the Dunkirk beaches, was now all but over, and although No 43 Sqn had only encountered the enemy once, on 1 June, it was nevertheless afforded the privilege of adding the battle honour 'Dunkirk' to its squadron colours.

Although the shattered remnants of the British Expeditionary Force had now returned home, fighting in France continued unabated, as No 43 Sqn discovered on 7 June. Ordered off with No 601 Sqn to patrol between Le Treport and Aumale, and deal with any enemy bombers interfering with Allied troops, Sqn Ldr Lott led 11 Hurricanes out across the English Channel. Only two were destined to return that evening. When the patrol was completed, the formation was under orders to land at Rouen-Boos, refuel and rearm and receive instructions for further operations. Flying with them operationally for the first, and last, time was Flt Lt Tom Rowland, the new 'B' Flight commander.

Over France, somewhere beyond Blangy, Lott spotted a Do 17 coming straight at them, and fearing a trap, he refused to let the squadron follow as it dived away. Craning his neck he searched for the Bf 109s that he felt sure were lurking above, and called a warning to No 601 Sqn but, unfortunately, they were on a different radio frequency. As the enemy fighters descended, Rowland's Hurricane (L2116 – Townsend's mount for his three victories on 3 and 22 February and 8 April) took several hits. The engine was knocked, filling the cockpit with smoke, and other strikes jammed the hood. In a second attack the pilot was hit in the foot by a cannon shell, although he managed to pull off a successful crash landing.

Not seen again after this engagement were Flg Offs 'Eddie' Edmonds (L1944) and 'Wilkie' Wilkinson (L1847 FT-J), who had both fought so bravely over Dunkirk just one week earlier. Lott managed to get in some inconclusive bursts at sundry Bf 109s in the melee as his number two, Sgt Hallowes (N2585 FT-U), latched onto one which Lott had attacked and was now turning towards him. As he did so, the sergeant pilot was himself hit from behind and his Hurricane set on fire.

Turning toward friendly territory and preparing to bale out, Hallowes was taken by surprise when one of the Messerschmitts overshot his crippled Hurricane. Dropping back into his seat, he opened fire and claimed as destroyed yet another Bf 109, before he too took to his parachute.

Extricating themselves from the scrap, the remnants of the unit put down on a bomb-scarred Rouen-Boos airfield and counted heads. Four pilots were missing, and Sgt Buck had burst a tyre on landing and was now out of the fray.

From Rouen-Boos the surviving pilots departed for another field, where they refuelled and rearmed before joining up with No 1 Sqn to cover Blenheims in the Abbeville/Amiens area. Again, incompatible radio frequencies meant no inter-squadron communications, and the units parted when No 1 wrongly assumed that No 43 was headed back for England.

The Blenheims were not seen, but spotting a formation of enemy bombers, escorted by Bf 109s and Bf 110s (40+ in total), heading south-west along the coast, Lott led No 43 in to attack. Individual fights developed across the sky, and Lott expended his ammunition on a Bf 109 which he followed down to a crash-landing in a big swirl of dust. His magazines empty, and with the rest of the squadron nowhere to be seen, he headed back for Tangmere. There, he found only John Simpson with a

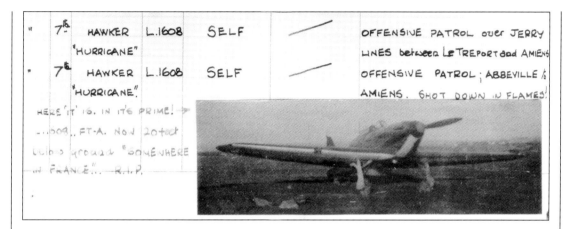

| " | 7ᵗʰ | HAWKER<br>"HURRICANE" | L.1608 | SELF | —— | OFFENSIVE PATROL over JERRY<br>LINES between LeTREPORT and AMIENS |
| " | 7ᵗʰ | HAWKER<br>"HURRICANE". | L.1608 | SELF | —— | OFFENSIVE PATROL; ABBEVILLE /o<br>AMIENS. SHOT DOWN IN FLAMES! |

HERE 'IT' IS. IN IT'S PRIME! →
...1608, FT-A. NOW 20 feet
below ground "SOMEWHERE
IN FRANCE".. R.I.P.

bullet-holed Hurricane. Of the others, only Buck with his burst tyre was certainly safe. On this second engagement, Woods-Scawen was shot down and had baled out, 'Oleo' Ottewill had taken to his parachute severely burnt and Sgt Ayling had crash-landed his severely shot up Hurricane at Rouen-Boos. A grim day indeed.

Two days later an influx of new pilots from No 6 OTU bolstered the depleted squadron as Plt Offs J Cruttenden, D G Gorrie and James and Sgts G C Brunner, J P Mills and J L Crisp arrived at Tangmere. So too did Flg Off J F J Haworth and Sgt W T Pratt from No 25 Sqn (Blenheims). Pre-war No 22 Sqn Vildebeest pilot Flt Lt Tom Dalton-Morgan, fresh from an Air Ministry desk, also arrived to become the third 'B' Flight commander in as many weeks. A welcome addition was the return of a newly commissioned Frank Carey, a survivor of the virtual annihilation of No 3 Sqn in France that had included the loss of their respected CO, Sqn Ldr Pat Gifford DFC. All of the new boys, one way or another, would make their mark on the squadron in the coming weeks and months although, sadly, Sgt Pratt would last only until the 15th when he crashed into the sea in Hurricane N2615 during low flying practice attacks.

With No 43 Sqn so depleted, little operational work was done in the immediate aftermath of 7 June, although welcome news came through that Rowland, Ayling, Hallowes, Woods-Scawen and Ottewill were at least alive. Ayling found a 'very second-hand' Hurricane at Rouen-Boos and managed to fly it home on the 10th, with Hallowes and Wood-Scawen also finding their way back. Rowland and Ottewill, both injured, would not re-join. On 16 June, covered by Flg Offs Haworth and H C Upton, Sqn Ldr Lott carried out a reconnaissance of the Cherbourg Peninsula – a task which was to earn him a Mention in Despatches.

That same day, one of the new pilots, Plt Off F H James, crashed on landing at Tangmere, writing off Hurricane N2618 in the process. After 'landing' too high, the aircraft bounced, stalled and turned over. James ended up in the Royal West Sussex Hospital with severe concussion, but was probably lucky to be alive. Not until the 21st were the 'Fighting Cocks' again declared fully operational, although it was not until early July that the squadron would properly join the battle once again. Nonetheless, the posting to No 43 Sqn on 22 June of one of its pre-war Fury pilots, Sqn Ldr 'Tubby' Badger, for 'Supernumerary flying duties' would prove to be timely indeed.

Sgt 'Oleo' Ottewill was badly burned on 7 June 1940 having baled out of his Hurricane (L1608 FT-A) during the ill-fated squadron patrol over France on that day. This is an extract from Pete Ottewill's Log Book, in which he writes under the photograph of L1608 that it was now buried '20 feet below ground "SOMEWHERE IN FRANCE" . . . R.I.P.'

# THE BATTLE OF BRITAIN

The squadron that had returned to Tangmere just one month ago looked a very different unit come 1 July. Old faces had gone, some forever, and many of the Hurricanes with which No 43 had started the war had been lost, but as George Lott observed, 'New faces and new aeroplanes, but the same old spirit'. Certainly a sense of renewed purpose prevailed on the squadron, and at Tangmere generally, with the realisation that things were now, more than ever before, critical.

However, activity seemed limited when July got underway, with repeated convoy patrols and the occasional scramble to intercept an anti-climatic 'X' plot being the regular daily round. In a break from the routine, the unit escorted Blenheims to France twice on the 1st. Three days later South African Plt Off Johannes Oelofse made a forced landing at Tangmere in P3468, and although the Hurricane was repaired on the squadron, it was the same aeroplane which was destined to carry him to his death a little over a month later.

One month exactly since that fateful day over France, No 43 Sqn got at last to fire its guns in anger once more, albeit that the Do 17 engaged over Beachy Head by Plt Offs Brunner and Cruttenden and Sgt Buck escaped into cloud. The engagement was inconclusive, but as they returned to base Cruttenden's engine caught fire and filled the cockpit with smoke and fumes. On pushing his head and shoulders out of the cockpit to see, Cruttenden was sucked out by the slipstream and landed in a field just 20 yards away from where his Hurricane (L1849) ended its days. The location was north-east of Bognor Regis, not far from Tangmere.

On 9 July the same pilot had another accident when landing at Tangmere in L1824 after failing to properly manipulate the flap selector, stalling and crashing through the boundary hedge. It was noted that whilst this was a case of pilot error, there should be no disciplinary action as the shock of baling out of a burning Hurricane two days previously may have affected Cruttenden's judgment. But this was not the only Hurricane to be lost by the squadron that day.

During the late morning Red Section were scrambled to intercept an incoming raid off the Isle of Wight. Sqn Ldr Lott was Red 1 (P3464), with Plt Off Carey Red 2 and Sgt Mills Red 3. The three Hurricane pilots found twelve distant specks, and pushing up his goggles for better vision, Lott identified them as six Ju 87s and six Bf 110s. As they closed on their quarry, the Stukas slid into cloud and the Bf 110s wheeled round to meet the Hurricanes face-on. Lott takes up the story;

'Jousting like a couple of knights of old, we rushed at each other head on. At 300 yards I pressed the firing button and at that very instant there was a terrific SPANG! I felt a blow in my face and right eye. Too late I remembered that I had left my goggles up. A smell of escaping coolant

Sqn Ldr John Vincent Clarence 'Tubby' Badger took command of No 43 Sqn when Sqn Ldr Lott was shot down and wounded on 9 July 1940. Badger had been posted to No 43 Sqn for supernumerary flying duties on 22 June 1940, but was no stranger to the unit. He had first joined the 'Fighting Cocks' on 15 July 1933, after graduating from RAF College, Cranwell. Flying Furies as a 21-year-old pilot officer, Badger spent a little over a year with No 43 Sqn before transferring to the School of Naval Co-operation in 1934. He went to sea with 821 Naval Air Squadron, equipped with Fairey Seal and Shark observation reconnaissance biplanes from the deck of HMS *Courageous*, the following year, and eventually joined the Maritime Aircraft Establishment at Felixstowe in 1937. Badger remained here until ordered back to Fighter Command, and No 43 Sqn, in June 1940. Badger enjoyed great success in his seven weeks as CO, claiming eight and two shared kills, one probable and two damaged. When he was shot down, wounded, over Woodchurch, in Kent, on 30 August, he crashed through tall trees in his parachute and was impaled on a broken bough and further horribly injured. Taken to Ashford Hospital, Badger endured terrible pain and suffering for many months before finally succumbing to his injuries on 30 June 1941 in the RAF Hospital at Halton. He was 29 years old. His DFC was announced on 6 September 1940, with the following words;

'This officer assumed command of a squadron in July 1940, and it is through his personal leadership that the squadron has achieved so many successes since the intensive air operations began. He has been instrumental in destroying six enemy aircraft. In spite of the fact that on three occasions he has returned with his aircraft very badly damaged through enemy cannon fire, he has immediately taken off in another aircraft to lead his squadron on patrol. Sqn Ldr Badger has displayed great courage and resolution.'

This photograph was taken soon after 'Tubby' Badger, also Mentioned in Despatches, graduated from the RAF College in 1933 with the coveted Sword of Honour

filled the cockpit as I keeled over and, corkscrewing hard, dived for cloud cover. On the way down I called Reds 2 and 3 and told them that I was hit and out of it.

'Although I was inwardly raging, I was still thinking clearly, and arranged to enter the cloud on a northerly heading which would take me to the nearest land. I put my hand over my left eye. All I could see was a white opaqueness. I was blind in the right eye. I was losing coolant from the engine and plenty of blood from my face, and didn't know if I would pass out or the engine seize up, so I prepared for a quick bale out. I undid my harness, slid back the hood and unlatched the side panel.

'I told base of the current state of affairs and said that I might have to bale out at any moment. The controller, David Lloyd, called "OK Red 1. Don't worry. We'll send a boat out". I knew as well as David that there was no boat to send, but I also knew that it was meant as a message of good cheer and support. I eased up to give myself a little more baling space and stayed on my northerly heading until I saw the corner of Langstone Harbour. I called for a vector to Tangmere and got "Steer 090. Keep it up!" Tangmere was not far, and I began to hope that I could make it. David told me that I was three miles north of base, so I turned south and let down through the cloud.

'The engine was now very rough, and I hoped and expected to see Tangmere when I came out of cloud at 800 ft. To my dismay I found that

Scotsman Plt Off David Gorrie joined No 43 Sqn at Tangmere in early July 1940, and was one of the pilots involved in shooting down the He 111 at Hipley on 12 July 1940. He also claimed a Bf 109 destroyed on 6 September, but had left the squadron before the end of the year. He was killed on 4 April 1941 in a mid-air collision whilst serving as an instructor with No 2 FTS at Brize Norton. This shot of him standing beside his Hurricane was taken at Tangmere on 13 July 1940, the day after his first combat (shared) claim

Taking the 'official' start date of the Battle of Britain as 10 July 1940, this was No 43 Sqn's first claim – He 111 G1+FA of *Stab*/KG 55, shot down by Sqn Ldr Badger, Flt Lt Dalton-Morgan, Plt Offs de Mancha, Gorrie and Upton and Sgt Ayling close to The Horse & Jockey pub in Hipley, Hampshire. Oberleutnant Kleinhanns was killed in the attack, but the remaining four crew were captured. Percy Tibble, landlord of the pub, took the German airmen into captivity armed with a toy pistol!

I was over Arundel and way off to the east. I had overshot. Turning back towards base, my propeller finally stopped dead and I was down to 700 ft. There was nothing for it, the engine was burning, I couldn't see through the starred windscreen and my harness was undone. I heaved myself over the side and without waiting streamed my parachute. I had no time to check a swing which developed and before I knew it I had landed on my back in the middle of a road which turned out to be the main road at Fontwell. Two men ran to me from a van which had stopped nearby. Blood soaked and gasping for breath, I must have looked in a bad way. They asked me if I was alright. I just nodded. I couldn't speak.'

But George Lott was far from alright for he had been permanently blinded in the right eye, thus ending his operational flying career. With immediate effect, Sqn Ldr John Badger assumed command.

In an interesting sequel to this mission, the Air Ministry later decided that the Battle of Britain 'officially' commenced on 10 July – the day after George Lott's escapade. Thus he failed to qualify as a Battle of Britain pilot, and was not awarded the coveted Battle of Britain clasp. As he would later laconically remark, 'Nobody had told the Germans that the Battle of Britain hadn't started yet!' However, Lott was awarded the Distinguished Flying Cross (DFC) for his leadership of No 43 Sqn, and before the end of 1940 would also be bestowed with the Distinguished Service Order (DSO).

Sqn Ldr Badger was able to make his mark on his new unit just three days later when he led Flt Lt Dalton-Morgan and Plt Offs R A de Mancha, Gorrie and Upton and Sgt Ayling in repeated attacks on a He 111 of *Stab*/KG 55, which they eventually shot down near The Horse & Jockey Pub in Hipley, with one of the crew dead and another wounded. Later, the pilots visited the scene to view the Heinkel and collect souvenirs.

On 19 July there was a blow to squadron morale when the much-liked Sgt James Buck was killed. Patrolling along the South Coast between Selsey Bill and Bognor, the unit was jumped by about 15 Bf 109s of III./JG 27 and No 43 Sqn was to come out of the ensuing scrap rather badly. Flt Lt John Simpson (P3140) was hit and baled out over Worthing and landed, wounded, in a cucumber frame, although he had first claimed a Bf 109 as destroyed. The wreckage of his Hurricane was later recorded at Angmering-on-Sea. Simpson would not return to the squadron until November. Buck (P3531) baled out over the sea with a bullet wound in his leg, but drowned before he could swim ashore. Remembering this

action, Frank Carey recalled formating on Buck's inverted Hurricane, flying along quite steadily, but with nobody in the cockpit.

On the 20th two more Hurricanes were lost, resulting in yet another fatality. Yellow Section, patrolling over Convoy *Bosom*, went to investigate a 'He 115' marked with a red cross. As Flg Off Joe Haworth approached in P3964, he was seen to suddenly pull away and then bale out, although his body was never found. He had apparently been hit by defensive fire from the aeroplane, which was marked with the international red cross symbol and carried the German civilian code D-AKAR.

The Heinkel (in fact a He 59 of *Seenotflugkdo* 1) was subsequently shot down by Flg Offs M D Doulton and T E Hubbard and Plt Off T Grier of No 601 Sqn, No 43's Tangmere neighbours. None of the crew survived.

The other squadron aircraft lost on this day was Hurricane P3784 FT-U, flown by Sgt Jim Hallowes. Soon after taking off from Tangmere on patrol, Hallowes was alarmed to see the oil pressure in his engine drop, followed by the inevitable seizure of the fighter's Rolls-Royce Merlin. He was forced to make a good wheels-up landing in a small meadow at Amberley, near Arundel, in West Sussex. What he did not know at the time was that the engine failure had been caused by a lack of oil in the Merlin.

Hearing about the crash, and realising with horror that he had forgotten to check, or top up, the oil during the Daily Inspection, the flight sergeant in charge of Hallowes' aeroplane drove out to Amberley and filled up the oil tank – explaining to the Army guard that it was to stop the engine corroding before the Hurricane was collected! The soldiery, ignorant of anything to do with aero engines, of course believed him, and the subterfuge was never discovered. Flt Lt Sharman, the unit's Engineering Officer, remained unable to put a finger on the cause of the accident!

On the 21st, during yet another convoy patrol, Sqn Ldr Badger was hit by a cannon shell in the starboard aileron of his usual mount, Hurricane P3971. He managed to limp back home despite the fact that the aileron

Flt Lt John Simpson was yet another of the No 43 Sqn Fury pilots who went on to fly Hurricanes with the unit during the early stages of the war. He achieved success during the actions over the north-east, Dunkirk, France and the Battle of Britain, before being shot down and wounded on 19 July. Simpson was still recovering from his injuries (including a broken collar bone) when this photograph was taken during his attendance at Buckingham Palace for the investiture of his DFC. He left No 43 Sqn to take command of No 245 Sqn at Aldergrove, Northern Ireland, in December 1940. From June 1941 Simpson fulfilled staff jobs, and was still serving in the RAF post-war. On 12 August 1949 he committed suicide by shooting himself in Hyde Park, London, whilst still in the service, and was buried at St Andrews Churchyard, Tangmere. A book about Simpson's exploits was written by his friend Hector Bolitho and published during the war. Called *Combat Report*, it was a classic tale of an RAF fighter pilot's life in the early years of World War 2

At approximately 0740 hrs on 20 July 1940 this No 43 Sqn Hurricane (P3784 FT-U) lost all oil pressure and its engine seized up. The pilot, Sgt Hallowes, made a very skilful wheels-up forced landing in a meadow at Amberley. By 1200 hrs the same day, Hallowes was flying again on ops from Tangmere. This machine had already flown from 0425 to 0615 hrs that morning, and for nearly two hours the night before, and there are grounds for believing that that the oil tank had not been checked, although the Form 700 had been signed to that effect. Shortly after the crash Flt Sgt Savage of 'B' Flight went to the scene with four gallons of used oil and poured it into the aircraft's tank, proclaiming in a loud voice for the benefit of the Army guard, 'This will stop the engine from corroding until they come to pick it up'. Hallowes, it seems, never became aware of the circumstances surrounding his forced landing, or the subsequent subterfuge!

Joining No 43 Sqn straight from No 6 OTU on 6 July 1940, with but few hours on Hurricanes, Plt Off Ricardo de Mancha (whose father was Italian and mother English) was thrown into action on 21 July 1940 with virtually no combat experience. Ten miles south of The Needles his Hurricane collided with a Bf 109 from 7./JG 27 flown by Leutnant Kroker. Both pilots were killed in the impact. The picture of this young and inexperienced 23-year-old flier, with his pretty girlfriend, very much epitomises the fighter pilot of 1940

had partially jammed and the aeroplane was very difficult to control (it was possibly this episode that earned Badger a Mention in Despatches). Sadly, Plt Off Ricardo de Mancha, who had only joined the unit on 6 July, collided with a Bf 109 during the same combat south of The Needles and was killed. July had not been a particularly auspicious month for No 43 Sqn, and it was perhaps not surprising that on the 23rd it was withdrawn to Northolt for a period of what the Operations Record Book called 'rest'.

Two days after arrival at Northolt Plt Off Roy Lane took Hurricane N2665 through the boundary hedge after overshooting, and on the 28th the squadron was sent down to Hawkinge for the Dover patrol – so much for the rest! Indeed, the remainder of July saw No 43 Sqn shuttling to and from Northolt and Hawkinge on a daily basis to carry out patrols, and on the 29th Plt Off Campbell was killed force landing L1944 following engine failure. On 1 August HQ Fighter Command considered that No 43 Sqn had taken sufficient rest and ordered it back to Tangmere.

The first significant action of August took place on the 8th. Convoy *Peewit*, steaming westwards down the English Channel, attracted a good deal of Luftwaffe attention, and many of the No 11 Group Sqns were called upon to deal with the attacks, not least of all No 43. Ordered off at 1540 hrs, 12 aircraft were vectored south of the Isle of Wight to patrol over the convoy, whereupon a large formation of enemy aircraft was encountered at around 20,000 ft. Inevitably, a huge scrap ensued, and three Ju 87s, a Bf 109 and a Bf 110 were confirmed by No 43 Sqn, along with another seven Ju 87s and three Bf 109s 'unconfirmed'. One of the latter had been attacked by Sqn Ldr Badger in P3971, although he broke off his attack when the oxygen panel on his Hurricane came adrift and flew off, causing Badger to think that he had been hit by cannon fire.

On the debit side, though, the squadron came back without Plt Offs Oelofse and Cruttenden in P3468 and P3781 (FT-O), respectively. Also downed at Ford Farm, Whitwell, on the Isle of Wight, was Plt Off H Upton in P3267, although he was uninjured. Frank Carey and Tony Woods-Scawen both landed back at Tangmere both with badly shot-up Hurricanes and slight wounds. Carey's aeroplane had a hole blown in the port wing 'big enough for a man to crawl through' after a 20 mm round exploded all of his ammunition in that wing. No trace of Cruttenden was ever found, although the body of Oelofse was later washed ashore and buried by his brother officers at St Andrews Church, Tangmere.

The weather gave a slight respite to activities over the next three days, although by the 12th the Luftwaffe was back over the Channel again, allowing No 43 Sqn to claim a Ju 88 'probable' by Carey and three He 111s 'damaged' by Upton in mid Channel and south of Worthing. Sgt A L M Deller, flying R4108, experienced engine failure and made a wheels-up forced landing upon returning to Tangmere, whilst Plt Off Woods-Scawen's Hurricane (R4110) had taken six hits in the engine and oil tank. Deller, participating in his first combat, later wrote;

'We seemed to take forever to climb to 21,000 ft, then someone shouted "Here come the bastards" and there was a terrific noise of gunfire. I was then in the middle of a lot of aircraft and my Hurricane was hit in the engine. Glycol and oil were all over the windshield, and I couldn't see anything so I spun down out of the area, recognised Selsey Bill, and coasted back to the airfield and landed wheels up.'

The next day, however, saw a major spate of activity with both victories and losses being experienced as No 43 Sqn scrambled before breakfast to meet a large formation of Ju 88s, Bf 109s and Bf 110s approaching from the south near Littlehampton. Sgt Mills claimed hits on a Bf 109 which may well have been the *Stab* I./JG 2 machine of *gruppen* adjutant Oberleutnant Paul Temme, which bellied in near Shoreham Airport. Sqn Ldr Badger claimed two Ju 88s damaged and saw one crash into Swanbourne Lake, Arundel, as three parachutes descended nearby. Another, hit and set smoking by Hallowes, may well have been the Ju 88 which crashed at Treyford. The enemy bombers were from *Stab* II./KG 54 and *Stab* I./KG 54 respectively.

On the down side, though, Flt Lt Tom Dalton-Morgan was hit by cross fire from the enemy bombers and baled out of Hurricane P3972 over Cocking Down, injuring his ankle in the jump. Luckier was Sgt Dennis

Sgt Alan Deller joined No 43 Sqn with Dennis Noble on 3 August 1940, and nine days later made a forced landing at Tangmere following combat over the English Channel. He had gone into action with only ten hours on Hurricanes from his time at the OTU, and less than two hours local flying with his flight commander. On 7 September he was again shot down, baling out unhurt over Babylon Farm, Sutton Valence, Kent. Following his use of an Irvin Air Chute on that day, Alan Deller became a member of the 'Caterpillar Club' – an exclusive club for airmen whose lives had been saved by Irvin parachutes

Relaxing outside one of the dispersal huts at Tangmere during August 1940, these No 43 Sqn pilots all took part in the battles over the south coast during the course of that month. Two of them did not survive. They are, standing left to right, Sgt Noble, Plt Off Upton, Plt Off Gorrie, Plt Off van den Hove d'Ertsenrijck and Sgt Hallowes, kneeling, Plt Off du Vivier, and seated, Sqn Ldr Badger

Noble, who left the battle streaming a white banner of glycol but managed to make it back. His Hurricane, V7221, was out of action until the 15th while it underwent an engine block change. Of this, his first engagement, young Noble wrote to his sister telling her that seven bullet holes were found in his Hurricane, but that he was okay, although he had been covered in coolant. Of the Hurricane he said, 'They are marvellous machines, and I would take on anything in one'.

Plt Off Woods-Scawen, also hit by the German gunners, managed to jump clear of his Hurricane after force landing at Northend Farm, Milland. Woods-Scawen escaped just as Hurricane R4102 erupted in flames, and despite the best efforts of Petworth Fire Brigade the aeroplane was lost.

A further scramble at 1600 hrs saw ten squadron Hurricanes ordered off to patrol the Isle of Wight, where a returning force of Ju 88s was encountered and Sgt Hallowes executed a 'frightening' head on attack. In the same combat Hallowes claimed a Do 17 that he followed down to crash in a small wood by Thorness Bay, Isle of Wight. His account of the incident is very precise and detailed. However, no known German loss fits this claim, and there are no matching recorded incidents on the ground or even near the spot so accurately pin-pointed by Hallowes. Doubtless this will remain one of those unsolved mysteries of the 1939-45 air war.

Two separate engagements during the late afternoon and early evening of the 14th saw a He 111 of III./KG 27 sent into the sea off the Isle of Wight, seven squadron pilots having had a hand in its demise, and another He 111 (also of III./KG 27) engaged in the Selsey area and pursued out to sea. Sgt Herbert Montgomery, flying Hurricane L1739 FT-Q, failed to return from the chase that continued in and out of squally clouds and ended some 40 miles south of Beachy Head. Although the squadron only claimed this as 'damaged', it would not have the satisfaction at the time of knowing that the Heinkel had failed to make it home. The body of Montgomery, who had only joined from No 6 OTU 11 days earlier, was washed ashore on the French coast.

15 August, although a busy day, thankfully saw no No 43 Sqn losses. Red Section pilots lined up for target practice on a Ju 88 from LG 1 that

Sergeants' Mess,
RAF Station,
TANGMERE,
Sussex

19 August 1940

Dear Phyl,
I expect that Ma has already told you that I am with a fighter squadron on the south coast and what a hot spot it is too. We are the busiest sector in the group at the moment. For five days a week we have to stay on the camp all day and every day and the sixth is free for us to go out where we please. Even so we never get away on time, for the Hun has a bad habit of having

raids about a quarter to one, which means a couple of hours' hard work and a late dinner. Our day is from one-o'clock to one-o'clock, and so I am able to go to London and spend the evening with Marie. It makes a very pleasant and welcome break. We work more or less 24 hours a day, and it is pretty tiring. When we are not intercepting raids we are patrolling convoys, and believe me it is hard going. Anyway, I like it all the same, plenty of larking about which suits me to the ground. I still fly Hurricanes and would not change for anything. I think that they are marvellous machines and would tackle anything in one.

The first day I went into battle I was shot down. I had seven holes in the machine, but I was okay. One bullet went into the radiator which caused the coolant to leak and I came down with streams of white smoke from the engine. I was covered in the stuff too. Anyway, I learned more in those few minutes then ever before. It was a fine experience. I shot down my first machine last Friday, a dive-bomber. The day before, seven of us shot down a lone bomber. As there were seven of us no one could hardly claim it. Yesterday I attacked another dive-bomber, and just as I was about to strike the decisive blow my guns failed to work. Fortunately I was able to dive away before I was caught napping, but I got a bullet in each wing. All that was due to the carelessness of a rigger who had failed to check the air system. I played hell when I came down. When I went up again it was too late as they had gone.

Well I must close now Phyl, so cheerio and all the best.

Your loving brother Dennis.

*This was the last letter home from No 43 Sqn pilot Sgt Dennis Noble. Eleven days later he was dead, shot down in his Hurricane over Hove, in Sussex.*

**Sgt Dennis Noble, a 20-year-old from Retford, Nottinghamshire, joined No 43 Sqn on 3 August 1940, but was dead before the end of the month, killed when he was shot down over Hove by a Bf 109 on the 30th. His last letter home, written to his sister Phyl, is a poignant reminder of one of 'the Few'**

they finally shot down at Southbourne, West Sussex. Frank Carey described it as a 'sitting duck', but Sqn Ldr Badger returned with hits in the canopy behind his head, through the airscrew, glycol pipe and ignition leads, and with one bullet in the heel of his shoe! Woods-Scawen also claimed a He 111 that he sent into the sea trailing smoke, but returned yet again with bullet holes in his Hurricane. The next day, though, would prove to be one of No 43 Sqn's hardest fought of the whole war.

Plt Off Frank Carey's Combat Report for 16 August perhaps best sums up the drama of the day;

This solitary Ju 88 had provided shooting practice for No 43 Sqn pilots on 15 August 1940 when it was brought down at Priors Leaze, Southbourne. In all, some seven pilots took shots at the bomber before it crashed. Oberleutnant Moller and Gefrieter Anders were both killed, although the remaining two members of the crew survived the forced landing to be captured. Before crashing, one of the gunners on board the Ju 88 had scored hits on Sqn Ldr Badger's Hurricane

'I was leading "A" Flight (in Hurricane R4109) behind the leader of the squadron, having taken off at 1245 hrs. We were patrolling Selsey Bill at 11,000 ft when I gave the Tally-Ho on sighting waves of Ju 87s. The leader ordered the squadron to attack one formation of '87s from the front, and immediately on closing the leader of the enemy aircraft was hit by the squadron leader and the crew baled out.

'I pulled my flight over to the left to attack the right hand formation as we met them. Almost as soon as I opened fire the enemy aircraft's crew baled out and crashed in the sea, just off Selsey Bill. I turned to continue my attack from the rear as the enemy aircraft had been completely broken up by the frontal attack, and several other waves behind them turned back out to sea immediately, although we had not attacked them. I picked out one Ju 87 and fired two two-second bursts at him and the enemy aircraft burst into flames at the port wing root.

'I did not wait to see it crash as I turned to attack another. After one burst at the third enemy aircraft two large pieces of metal broke off the port wing and it seemed to stop abruptly and go into a dive. I did not see it crash as two other Ju 87s were turning onto my tail.

'I eventually picked on a fourth, but after firing two bursts and causing the engine to issue black smoke the enemy aircraft turned out to sea and I ran out of ammunition. Noticing fire behind me, I turned to see a pair of Me 109s behind me, one firing and the other apparently guarding his tail. After a few evasive actions the enemy aircraft broke off and I returned to land and re-fuel and re-arm at 1340 hrs. During the attacks I noticed many enemy aircraft jettisoning their bombs into the sea.'

When he landed back at Tangmere, Carey found a battered and smoking ruin. The airfield had been badly hit by those Ju 87s of *Stukageschwader* 2 that had managed to penetrate the defensive fighter screen, but as Carey later observed;

'Due to our positioning, we were only able to fire on about the second wave, leaving the leaders more or less undisturbed in their bombing. However, we were very lucky that our head on attack so demoralised the Ju 87s that they, and the successive waves behind them, broke up. Some dropped their bombs in the sea in an effort to get away.'

Without doubt, therefore, the damage at Tangmere would have been much more serious were it not for the fighter interceptions – albeit that fighter units other than No 43 Sqn were also involved in the fight.

At Tangmere, a number of squadron Hurricanes were lost in the bombed hangars, and AC 1 Young, a 19-year-old No 43 Sqn flight mechanic, was one of the fatalities on the ground. Two other Hurricanes were also lost, but the pilots were safe. Plt Off Woods-Scawen had to put Hurricane N2621 down at Parkhurst, on the Isle of Wight, after claiming

This was one of the Tangmere-raiding Ju 87 Stukas of 3./StG 2, shot down beside the B2145 road at Selsey on 16 August 1940 by Sqn Ldr J V C Badger. The two crew were captured, both having suffered terrible wounds

The aftermath of the bombing raid on Tangmere on 16 August 1940. This shot shows one of the collapsed buildings, with destroyed No 43 Sqn transport inside. Although the squadron gave a good account of itself in the air against the attacking Stukas, it lost a number of Hurricanes on the ground when one of its hangars was hit. Amongst those killed on the ground was No 43 Sqn's AC 1 Young, a 19-year-old flight mechanic

two Ju 87s, and Plt Off Upton crash-landed P3216 near Selsey after its oil system was holed by return fire from a Ju 87.

Later that day there was another Hurricane loss when Sgt Crisp baled out of Hurricane L1736 FT-H near Bognor. His Log Book records, 'Beat up with five '109s. Baled out and broke leg (starboard)'.

Despite the day's losses there had been significant successes, although a tally of the Stukas claimed by No 43 Sqn reaches 24, with six probables. Without a doubt there is a significant element of overclaiming here, but all of the squadron pilots airborne in that battle shot at (and quite probably hit) at least one Ju 87. More often than not they may have been unaware of other pilots shooting at the same victim, or may have attacked aircraft which were already going down. Certainly, it was a hectic battle and over-claiming was to be expected. What is certain is that No 43 Sqn had acquitted itself well.

After the rigours of 16 August, the next day was comparatively restful. However, Sgt Jim Hallowes (who had also been in action on the 16th, claiming three Ju 87s destroyed) was part of Blue Section which was ordered off to investigate an unidentified plot over Winchester. The others in the section were Sqn Ldr Badger and Plt Off David Gorrie. At nearly 30,000 ft, Hallowes spotted a Do 17 and pursued it, firing, into a full throttle and ever steepening dive. At 12,000 ft a terrific vibration set up in the Hurricane and Hallowes noted that the ASI (air speed indicator) was off the clock at over 400 mph. Fabric was tearing from the ailerons and control surfaces, and fighting with the controls, Hallowes managed to pull out at 5000 ft and the Dornier was nowhere to be seen.

Upon Hallowes' return to Tangmere, it was found that Hurricane V6533 had been over-stressed and the mainplane root fittings bent

**No 43 Sqn's hangar burns furiously after the attack on Tangmere on 16 August 1940**

backwards. A technical team from Hawkers inspected the damaged airframe and concluded that a speed of 620 mph had been reached. Hallowes himself had experienced a damaged ear drum in the excessive dive, an injury which prevented him from later joining the Hawker company as a test pilot. Notwithstanding his injured ear, Hallowes was back in action the very next day.

18 August 1940 has, quite rightly, been described as the hardest fought day of the Battle of Britain. It was certainly so for the pilots and groundcrew of No 43 Sqn, who found themselves in a hectic routine of patrol, land, refuel and scramble throughout the day. As with the 16th, this day's primary action involved a battle against Stukas. At 1430 hrs 28 Ju 87s of StG 77 attacked RAF Thorney Island, and were intercepted by the Hurricanes of Nos 43 and 601 Sqns. Just as the Combat Report for Carey summed up the actions of the 16th, so does that of Jim Hallowes for the 18th. However, Carey himself (a mere pilot officer) was actually leading the squadron on this day. Hallowes reports;

'We took off at 1410 hrs and climbed to 15,000 ft, and a few minutes later sighted a large formation of Ju 87s at about 10,000 ft, with a fighter escort of Me 109s circling above at about 18,000 ft – the latter appeared to peel off and head towards Portsmouth and the balloon barrage whilst the Ju 87s went into line-astern formation and headed for Thorney Island.

'I followed Blue Leader in line astern but lost sight of him as we engaged the enemy. I caught up with one formation of five Ju 87s in line astern, opened fire at about 300 yards, and two people baled out of the No 5 machine and a further two from the No 4 machine, both aircraft going into a dive about three to four miles east of Thorney Island.

'I then carried out a quarter attack on a third Ju 87 without any apparent result. Observing another Ju 87 at about 200 ft, which had released its bombs on Thorney Island, I came up into a position astern and gave it three short bursts. I was closing too fast and had to break away to the right, coming in again for a beam attack on the same machine, which broke in two just in front of the tail fin and fell in the Solent about halfway between the mainland and the Isle of Wight.

'I then spotted a Hurricane which was closing in astern of a Ju 87, with a Me 109 coming up in turn behind the Hurricane. The Hurricane turned left and I was in a good position for a beam attack on the Me 109. I could clearly see my bullets entering the fuselage from the nose to the tail and could see the holes as the Me 109 flashed past me about 100 yards ahead, going south. I heard the order to return to base, and being almost out of ammunition I returned, landed and rearmed. I claimed the Me 109 as damaged, but at a later date heard that an unclaimed Messerschmitt had crashed on the Isle of Wight and assumed it was the one I fired at.'

Officially, Hallowes was credited with three Ju 87s on 18 August in Hurricane P3386. This was the same aeroplane he had flown for the past ten days, and in which he had now claimed ten confirmed victories, two probables and one damaged. The Bf 109 referred to on the Isle of Wight was that flown by Oberleutnant Julius Neumann of 6./JG27, and at least one of the Ju 87s Hallowes claimed is likely to have been that flown by Oberleutnant Johannes Wilhelm which plunged into Fishbourne Creek.

No 43 Sqn losses that day were confined to Plt Off Frank Carey, who was hit in the right knee by a stray bullet. Told to stay away from

New Zealander Flg Off Harold North joined No 43 Sqn on 20 November 1939. His first victories came on 18 August when he downed a Ju 87 and claimed a second as a 'probable', followed by a He 111 on 26 August. During the latter action his aircraft was hit and he baled out wounded, his Hurricane crashing to the west of Chichester. After returning to the squadron upon recovery, he was then posted to No 96 Sqn and eventually to No 457 (RAAF) Sqn, with whom he was posted missing during an escort mission to Marquise on 1 May 1942

Plt Off Geoff Brunner, a pre-war sergeant pilot who had served with Nos 17 and 66 Sqns, joined No 43 Sqn on 10 June 1940. On 7 July he carried out a long low-level chase of a Do 17 across the English Channel until his ammunition ran out. On 26 August he claimed a He 111 as a 'probable' before his aircraft was hit and he was wounded in the ankle, making a wheels-up landing back at Tangmere. He did not return to operational flying, instead joining the A&AEE at Boscombe Down, ending the war with an AFC and Bar

Tangmere, where there were fears of more Stuka bombing, Carey had to crash-land Hurricane R4109 near Pulborough.

The next week or so turned out to be rather an anti-climax, and it was not until the 26th that things hotted up again for No 43 Sqn. On this day 12 No 43 Sqn aircraft were scrambled at 1600 hrs to patrol near Tangmere at 15,000 ft. Shortly after arriving on station a large formation of 100+ He 111s, escorted by 50 Bf 109s and Bf 110s, were spotted and the 'Tally-ho!' given. No 43 Sqn attacked a formation of He 111s head on, and in the process of splitting up this section the unit was itself scattered all across the sky. A huge battle followed as individual Hurricanes chased Heinkel bombers across West Sussex, Hampshire and along the Channel coast, and the fighter escorts in turn attempted to deal with the threat posed by the relative handful of No 43 Sqn aircraft.

Sqn Ldr Badger and Sgt Hallowes pursued one of the Heinkels, raking it with fire and forcing it down at Wick, near Littlehampton. Plt Off North caused a second bomber to crash at Waterlooville, both He 111s (from KG 55) making reasonable belly landings. However, these claims were not without cost, as four squadron pilots were shot down by either return fire or the fighter escorts.

Plt Off Roy Lane baled out of P3220 over Forestside and, very badly burned, landed upside down when his parachute harness burnt through, suspending him from his ankles. Plt Off Colin Gray also took to his parachute, and upon landing near Bosham he found himself staring down the barrel of a suspicious farmer's shotgun. Plt Off Harold 'Knockers' North, having just despatched a Heinkel, jumped out of his burning Hurricane near Birdham. Only slightly luckier was Plt Off Geoff Brunner, who was attacked by an unseen fighter near Bognor. Badly shot up, and with no engine, he glided in for a successful belly landing at Tangmere, although he was admitted to hospital with a bullet wound in his ankle.

The loss of four aircraft was tempered a little by the arrival that evening of new pilot Flt Lt 'Dickie' Reynell as a replacement flight commander. Australian Reynell had previously flown Furies with No 43 Sqn in 1932-34, and was posted to the unit on loan from Hawkers, where he was a Hurricane test pilot.

Little of any note occurred until 30 August, and this turned out to be yet another black day for the hard pressed squadron. At around noon, 12 No 43 Sqn aircraft were involved in dogfights across Kent and Sussex, and at 1150 hrs Hurricane P3179, flown by Sgt Pilot Dennis Noble, was shot

This was the He 111 (G1+GM Wk-Nr 2165) of 4./KG 55 shot down by Harold North on 26 August at Westbrook Farm, Waterlooville. Oberfeldwebel Hennecke baled out too low and was killed, although the remainder of the crew stayed in the aircraft and were captured following the forced landing. The Heinkel came down close to the farmhouse, and in the crash the tail and rear fuselage were ripped from the bomber. Harold North was still descending by parachute when the shaken survivors clambered from his 'kill'

Australian Flt Lt Richard Carew Reynell, known universally as 'Dickie', was another pre-war Fury pilot with No 43 Sqn, having served with the unit between 1931 and 1934. An accomplished aerobatic pilot, he participated in the International Air Meeting at Brussels in 1931. Later, in 1937, Reynell joined Hawkers as a test pilot, but was recalled to the RAF on the outbreak of war and seconded back to his former employer so as to continue his vital test duties, primarily on the Hurricane. On 26 August 1940 he joined No 43 Sqn for operational experience, and shot down a Bf 109 on 2 September before being killed in action five days later. Reynell is pictured here outside the 'A' Flight dispersal hut at Tangmere shortly before his death

Plt Off Roy Lane, son of the Mayor of Southampton, joined No 43 Sqn at Tangmere on 13 July, and was one of the pilots who claimed a Ju 87 on 18 August. Shot down over Forestside on 26 August, he was very badly burned, and became one of Sir Archibald McIndoe's 'Guinea Pig' patients. Upon recovering from his wounds, he became a catapult-Hurricane pilot, before being posted to India in late 1943. Once in-theatre, Lane volunteered to serve in Japanese-occupied Burma as an air liaison officer for the Chindits. Whilst there, he was forced down behind enemy lines when the engine failed in his Hurricane. Quickly captured, he was beheaded by the Japanese on 20 June 1944

down and powered vertically into the pavement of Woodhouse Road, Hove. Noble was taken home for burial in his native Retford, and there the sad story would otherwise have ended but for the fact that a private enthusiast excavated the crash site in 1997 and found substantial remains of the pilot. Distressingly for his family, an inquest had to be held as well as a second funeral. Perhaps there were sound reasons why other aviation archaeologists had for so long shunned this particular site?

As if the loss of Noble were not enough for one day, the commanding officer, Sqn Ldr Badger, was shot down and grievously wounded over the Ashford area at 1735 hrs. Baling out, but with severe wounds, Badger crashed through tall trees before falling onto the lawn of Townland Farm, Woodchurch, where the lady occupier gently tended to him. His Hurricane, V6548, screamed into the earth at Cuckolds Corner, near Bethersden. Despite immediate first aid, and hospital care, 'Tubby' bravely endured his injuries before succumbing to them on 30 June 1941. Hearing of his death, May Munton wrote to Badger's father on 3 July;

'Dear Mr Badger,

'I feel I must write you a line to tell you how dreadfully grieved I am to see the death of your son in today's *Times*. You will not know who I am, but it was in my garden that your son landed when his machine was hit and he had to take to his parachute. He was so badly wounded that there was little we could do for him. His courage was absolutely amazing and I shall never forget it. I saw him a few times when he was in Ashford Hospital, and though he was so ill, he was always brave and smiling. Please do not bother to reply to this, but I did want to send you my sympathy.

'Yours sincerely,

'May F Munton.'

Badger's Log Book was signed off by Flt Lt C B Hull DFC, who now found himself to be the Officer Commanding No 43 Sqn. As if to emphasise his surprise at suddenly becoming CO, he followed the description of himself as 'Commanding No 43 Sqn' in the endorsement of Badger's log with four exclamation marks. He was destined to live for just another week, but led six Hurricanes against a raid attacking Beachy Head Chain Home Low radar site the day after taking command.

By comparison, the 1st was a quiet day, but events of 2 September were to further shake the battered spirit of No 43 Sqn. Over Ashford – the very same hunting ground that had so recently claimed Badger – three of the squadron's Hurricanes were shot out of the sky in a matter of seconds at around 1330 hrs.

The 'Fighting Cocks' popular stalwart, Plt Off Tony Woods-Scawen, parachuted from his burning Hurricane V7420 too low and fell to his death. He died unaware that his brother, Patrick, a flying officer with No 85 Sqn, had been killed in identical circumstances just the day before. V7420 crashed at Fryland, near Ivychurch.

**This photograph, albeit of very poor quality, is included for purely historical reasons as it was taken on 30 August 1940 in the village of Woodchurch, Kent. It depicts Sqn Ldr Badger descending over the rooftops after abandoning his Hurricane, and just before he crashed through the branches of trees at Townland Farm, mortally wounded**

Seven-kill ace Plt Off Tony Woods-Scawen is seen at Tangmere just a few days before his death in action on 2 September 1940. He is standing outside the 'A' Flight dispersal hut at Tangmere, where a chequered flag 'borrowed' from a car racing circuit flutters – proudly continuing the squadron's pre-war black and white chequers tradition. Seemingly indestructable, Woods-Scawen was shot down four times before being killed. This is the official Air Ministry account of the occasion when he was downed over France on 7 June 1940;

'Plt Off Woods-Scawen was Blue 2 No 43 Sqn in the section led by Sqn Ldr Lott on 7 June 1940 when numerous Me 109s and Me 110s were sighted at about 1830 hrs over Le Treport. He formed line astern behind his leader and dived after the quarry. The next thing he knew something hit his machine from behind and he headed his aircraft westward. But it became so hot that he was forced to bail out and landed somewhere well to the west of Dieppe. He trekked 20 miles to Bacqueville, where he fell in with a motorised transport unit who eventually took him to Rouen. The river was crossed by ferry just ahead of the advanced enemy units. The bridge had already been blown up. His recollection of the journey is hazy, as he was continually being bombed and spent a lot of his time sheltering in cellars. At Le Mans he fell in with No 73 Sqn, and travelled by train to Caen and Cherbourg, where he arrived six days after being shot down. He crossed to England the following day and arrived at his home station carrying his Mae West and parachute.

'Signed, Plt Off F J Cridlan, Intelligence Officer No 43 Sqn, to Intelligence, HQ 11 Group RAF Fighter Command'

Flg Off Carswell drifted down beneath his parachute, suffering from burns and shell splinters, while his Hurricane, P3786, crashed at Bell Corner, Old Romney. This incident signalled the end of the redoubtable 'Crackers'' flying career.

The third casualty of the mission was Belgian Plt Off Leroy du Vivier, who baled out wounded from Hurricane P3903 which in turn crashed, inverted, at Warehorne. Du Vivier was destined to make very much of a mark on No 43 Sqn in later months and years.

On the credit side, Sgt Jefferys shot down a 4./JG 2 Bf 109 over Cale Hill Park, Little Chart, and new boy 'Dickie' Reynell claimed another from the same unit, which came to earth at West Hythe. Writing home to his wife the next day, Reynell gave an account of his first and last claim;

'I got my first Me 109 yesterday morning, as you will have probably heard by now. I got his engine, and followed him until he crashed in a small field. The machine broke up completely, but I saw the pilot being helped away by a couple of farm hands. I don't know how he got out of it, but he did'.

Shaken, but otherwise unhurt, Reynell's victim was Unteroffizier von Stein, who now faced the safety of five years captivity. Reynell would be dead within the week.

As with the 1st, the 3rd was less hectic, allowing No 43 Sqn to catch its breath before another big battle on the 4th, when Caesar Hull led the unit into a large formation of Bf 110s over the Sussex coast just after lunchtime. Flt Lt Dalton-Morgan, freshly out of the sick bay, avenged his wounds by sending a Bf 110 down in flames north of Worthing and chasing another until it force-landed in a field near Shoreham. Sgt Jeffreys also downed a Bf 110 in a field, and Hull and Upton seriously damaged two more *Zerstörers*. A fourth Bf 110 was chased across the Channel by Belgian Plt Off van den Hove d'Ertsenrijck, who sent it crashing into the sea seven miles south of Brighton, although his Hurricane (L1386) was hit in return and he had to make an emergency landing at RAF Ford.

The Messerschmitts massacred by No 43 Sqn that day were from ZGs 2 and 76, although the multiple claims and losses make it difficult, with any certainty, to tie up individual 'kills'. Upon returning to base, the pilots were heartened to find that Irishman Flt Lt 'Killy' Kilmartin had been posted back to his old unit after a spell 'resting' as an instructor with No 5 OTU.

The next day, on the squadron's second scramble at 1505 hrs, 12 aircraft were ordered off in the direction of the Thames Estuary, and Sgt Alex Hurry claimed a definite Bf 109 which he saw crash near Appledore Railway Station on the edge of Romney Marsh (this engagement is depicted on the cover of this book). Over 50 years later the crash site was excavated, and the body of Leutnant Helmut Strobl of 5./JG 27 found in the wreck of the Messerschmitt claimed by Hurry in the following Combat Report;

'I was flying in Blue section as Blue 3 at 20,000 ft over Biggin Hill when Blue 1 turned and dived. I followed but lost him in thick haze and joined up with Blue 2 at 10,000 ft and climbed again to re-join the squadron. At 18,000 ft at 1605 hrs over Maidstone I sighted some 30-40 Me 109s heading west north-west at 15,000 ft. I climbed into the sun and gave the "Tally Ho!", then turned and dived on to the rear vic of five enemy aircraft. During my dive they turned south and I carried out a quarter attack on the outer enemy aircraft. The length of my burst was five seconds. The enemy aircraft half rolled and dived and I followed as the remaining four aircraft were turning to attack me. The enemy aircraft pulled out at 5000 ft and flew south. I caught him again 12 miles north-west of Dungeness and fired a burst of six seconds. He caught fire, half rolled and dived vertically into the ground near Appledore Station, about ten miles north-west of Dungeness. No attempt made at evasion. Enemy markings were dull green with white wingtips and silver *(sic)* undersurfaces. I did not see the pilot bale out. The weather was hazy with 4/10ths cloud at 17,000 ft. Visibility 12 miles.'

Oddly, Hurry's Bf 109 had been shot down on 5 September, it was found and recovered on 5 September (1986), Strobl's birthday was 5 September, his flying licence was dated 5 September and he was finally laid to rest in his native Austria on 5 September.

On the 6th 12 squadron pilots were involved in a running fight between Mayfield and Dungeness that saw five Bf 109s and a Bf 110 claimed as shot down and a Ju 88 and two Bf 109s damaged. The only confirmed kill was a Bf 109 sent into the sea by Tom Dalton-Morgan, although another Bf 109 got in some shots at the Welsh ace's Hurricane, one hit smashing the canopy and cutting him around the face. This time there were no No 43 Sqn losses. This would not be the case 24 hours later.

It was not until late afternoon, at around 1600 hrs, that nine Hurricanes of No 43 Sqn were scrambled to intercept a huge raid coming in over Kent. Led into the attack by Caesar Hull, six of the Hurricanes swept into the bombers whilst 'Killy' Kilmartin's section of three were told to ward off any fighters. It was all over in moments. Hull was last seen firing at a Do 17, and his charred remains were later discovered in the burnt out shell of Hurricane V6641, which crashed in the grounds of a boy's school in Purley. Hit over Blackheath, Reynell baled out of Hurricane V7257 but fell to his death when his parachute refused to open. Further to the south, Sgt Alan Deller managed to bale out of Hurricane V7309 when it was hit by cannon fire and burst into flames, the pilot descending over Sutton Valence. He subsequently recalled;

'I can remember there were very few pilots to fly that trip, and that I was No 3 to Kilmartin. Caesar Hull was leading the other section, and as we approached the London area it seemed the sky was full of enemy aircraft. "Killy" went up after the top cover and Hull went into the bombers. What happened next was just a blur – the section got split up and tangled with some Me 109s. I got caught with one on my tail, concentrating too much on the one in front. I was thinking "they told me not to follow him down"

Welshman Tom Dalton-Morgan joined No 43 Sqn as a flight lieutenant commanding 'B' Flight in June 1940, and subsequently went on to command the squadron. He achieved an impressive score of claims with the unit, although he was himself shot down and slightly injured on 13 August 1940. He was awarded the DFC in September 1940, with a Bar in May 1941. Awarded a DSO in May 1943, Dalton-Morgan was granted an OBE two years later. The flamboyant fighting cock emblem on the Hurricane's engine was applied to most squadron aircraft during late 1940 and into 1941

when I was hit by a hail of cannon fire and the Hurricane burst into flames. I spun out of the melee and got my hood open and baled out, landing in an apple orchard close to a Spitfire which had bellied in through some hop poles. When I got back I found that Reynell and Hull had been killed in that battle.'

Perhaps more than any others, the losses of Caesar Hull and Dick Reynell affected the squadron morale very badly. Perhaps they had taken just *too* much punishment? When he landed back at Tangmere on 7 September, an ashen faced Kilmartin could only mutter 'My God, my God'. It probably summed up the feelings of everyone else on the squadron. By evening, Tom Dalton-Morgan had become the new CO of No 43 Sqn, and the remnants of the unit received orders to retire back to the No 13 Group airfield at RAF Usworth, near Newcastle. Its place at Tangmere was taken by No 607 Sqn, which had flown south from Usworth on 1 September.

The pilots of No 43 Sqn had fought valiantly and suffered grievously, but could still take justifiable pride in their combat record.

By the end of this particular period in the squadron's history, the following decorations had been awarded to No 43 Sqn pilots;

| | |
|---|---|
| Sqn Ldr C G Lott | Distinguished Service Order |
| Sqn Ldr J V C Badger* | Distinguished Flying Cross |
| Flt Lt T F Dalton-Morgan | Distinguished Flying Cross |
| Sgt H J L Hallowes | Distinguished Flying Medal & Bar |

(*Sqn Ldr Badger was also Mentioned in Despatches on 22 July 1940)

This evocative and historic photograph was taken outside the Officers' Mess at RAF Tangmere at 1300 hrs on 7 September during Sqn Ldr Lott's first visit back to his old unit since being blinded in his right eye on 9 July 1940. Standing, from left to right, are Plt Off H C Upton, Plt Off A E A van den Hove d'Ertsenrijck and Plt Off D G Gorrie, whilst sitting, from left to right, are Plt Off S Cary (squadron adjutant), Flt Lt J I Kilmartin, Sqn Ldr C G Lott, Flt Lt R C Reynell and Sqn Ldr C B Hull. The latter two pilots were killed in action about three hours after this photograph was taken, and it can be seen that Hull, who had only taken command of No 43 Sqn seven days previously, had not yet had time to have a squadron leader's third ring sewn onto his tunic. Plt Off van den Hove d'Ertsenrijck was killed in action with No 501 Sqn on 15 September 1940

# 'BLITZ' TO DIEPPE

On 8 September 1940 12 weary pilots flew No 43 Sqn's remaining serviceable Hurricanes northwards, leaving a further four unserviceable aeroplanes that were still undergoing repairs to be ferried out of Tangmere over the next seven days. Things at RAF Usworth were destined to run at a much gentler pace, with the primary function of No 43 Sqn whilst it was rested being the working up of new pilots fresh from OTUs to operational readiness. During the Usworth period an astonishing total of more than 87 pilots were posted in for final training, before moving on to more actively operational squadrons 'down south'.

However, No 43 still continued to function as an operational unit, flying a large number of patrols, interceptions and fighter-night patrols during this period. Very often these would be flown by the more seasoned pilots on the squadron, but they also provided very useful hands-on active flying experience for the new OTU 'greenhorns'.

Irishman Flt Lt John Ignatius 'Killy' Kilmartin joined No 43 Sqn at Tangmere in January 1938, and was still with the unit when the war began. On 3 November 1939 he joined No 1 Sqn in France, where he quickly achieved ace status, but returned to No 43 Sqn on 4 September 1940 following a spell as an instructor with No 5 OTU. Kilmartin achieved further victories with No 43 Sqn but left the unit in April 1941. This photograph was taken some time after the squadron had been posted to Usworth in September 1940, Kilmartin posing alongside Hurricane FT-F (serial unknown) probably at Acklington circa March 1941

One of the intake of pilots that was sent straight to No 43 Sqn from an OTU in order to complete their training was Sgt Richardson, who arrived at Drem in 1941. He is photographed alongside FT-G, which is believed to be Hurricane IIB Z3265. Sqn Ldr Dalton-Morgan used this very machine to destroy a Ju 88 on 8 June and a He 111 on 11 July 1941 (*Chris Doll*)

On 4 October Czech pilot Sgt Josef Pipa joined the unit, and he would very soon become a valued member of the 'Fighting Cocks'. Although an experienced pre-war pilot, Pipa came through the usual No 6 OTU route, and had barely completed a week's flying on Hurricanes with the training unit prior to joining No 43 Sqn. Perhaps indicative of his lack of Hurricane experience, he was involved in an accident on 10 October in L2143. Landing in a high wind, Pipa bounced back up to a height of 20 ft, stalled the starboard wing, and landed heavily on one wheel, collapsing the undercarriage. It was an error of judgment, but then it was only his sixth Hurricane landing! There were, however, more serious accidents.

The first of these occurred on 24 October when No 6 OTU 'freshman' Sgt Donald Stoodley died on his first night flight. Difficult enough even for experienced pilots, night flying in a Hurricane proved to be too much for this 21-year-old with but few hours on type. Trying to land at 80 degrees to the flarepath, the pilot crashed into the dispersal area in Hurricane V7303. Having made six unsuccessful attempts to land, Stoodley shut the throttle at 300 ft, glided steeply and then pulled out at 50 ft, before stalling in.

Another ex-OTU sergeant pilot casualty was 20-year-old Leonard Toogood, who was killed when his Hurricane dived in from altitude while on an authorised aerobatic flight on 27 October. His fighter (L1963) crashed at Broomeyholme Farm, Congburn Dean, the pilot having possibly blacked out as a result of oxygen failure. The month ended with Sgt Malinowski (Polish) making a forced landing in P3357 and running into a ditch at Chirnside after his engine cut out in flight. This was the first month of 1940 that No 43 Sqn had not encountered the enemy, although as detailed above, there had been a spate of accidents and two fatalities.

No 43 Sqn had the rare distinction of having two brothers – Reg and Peter Thompson – serving together during the unit's long spell at Drem. This is Reg, who served as an AC 1 Aircraft Rigger . . .

. . . whilst brother Peter was a pilot officer, who came directly to No 43 Sqn from his OTU. He was later killed in action over Malta on 13 May 1941 whilst flying a Hurricane with No 261 Sqn

An unusual feature of No 43 Sqn from December 1940 was that, for a while at least, two brothers served together on the unit – one a rigger, the other a pilot. AC 1 Reg Thompson came to the squadron's groundcrew from No 59 OTU at Longtown, and shortly after being posted in was astonished to find that his brother, Plt Off Peter Thompson, had joined No 43 Sqn as a pilot under training. The pair were together for some two or three months, during which time Reg was taken flying by his brother in the squadron Magister.

Sadly, Peter Thompson did not survive the war. Having completed his operational training with No 43 Sqn, he then volunteered for special duties overseas. Joining HMS *Ark Royal* at Gibraltar, Thompson flew a Hurricane off the carrier to Malta, where he served with No 261 Sqn until 13 May 1941 when he was shot down and killed in Hurricane V7115.

November and December 1940 continued in similar vein, with yet more accidents – albeit non fatal. It was probably with some relief that the squadron bade farewell to 1940, with hopes that 1941 would see their fortunes revived.

20 January 1941 at last saw the promise of action when Plt Off Carey took off from Drem with Plt Off Tufnell as his number two to look for an 'X' raid off the coast near Dundee. Flying out low over the sea so as not to be seen above the cloud cover, the pair came across a Ju 88 near Bell Rock Lighthouse and gave chase. Managing to get fairly close and beneath the enemy before being spotted, Carey was able to get in one or two bursts before the bomber climbed frantically into the cloud. There followed a chase in and out of the overcast when Carey suddenly spotted Tufnell heading back to the coast. Calling him, he got no answer, but decided to continue the chase alone. He flew on for some 15 minutes far out to sea.

Breaking off the inconclusive engagement, Carey turned for home, where he discovered that his number two had been hit by return fire from the Ju 88. Injured, Tufnell had crashed Hurricane P3776 at Bankhead Farm, north of Aberdeen, having been blinded in one eye.

Two days later the squadron lost one of its longest serving and most valued pilots when Jim Hallowes DFM, now a pilot officer, was posted out to instruct at No 56 OTU at Sutton Bridge. As Sqn Ldr Dalton-Morgan noted, so solid and reliable a squadron member would be nigh on impossible to replace. Lost, too, was Sgt J R Stoker, who was killed when he crashed L1968 into the sea during air firing practice at Acklington. All the same, life continued, but on 7 February it must have seemed like déjà vu for Kilmartin as he watched Plt Off May go off to hunt down a stray barrage balloon in P3142 FT-N. Hardly such an adrenalin rush as engaging the enemy, but at least it afforded useful gunnery practice!

On the 11th, Plt Off Chris Doll had a fright in Hurricane P3809. He later gave an account of this episode and takes up the story;

'Before the war my Uncle Theo had been a vet, and I recall that one day I held an Alsatian dog whilst he put it down. "Don't worry" he said "if the dog pees before it dies. That's just normal and natural". Six years later those words came back to terrify me.

'On this day I was on a morning shipping patrol when a heavy mist came in from the sea and I was recalled to Drem. Before I got there the airfield was just about fogged in, and all I could see was a small corner of the field, so I opened the hood, put down the wheels and put down at

Three aces in the making. Photographed whilst at Drem during the spring of 1941, these three young pilot officers of No 43 Sqn were all destined to become aces, although none of them made any claims whilst serving with the 'Fighting Cocks'. They are, from left to right, Ray Harries, Chris Doll and Ron West, who scored 15 and 3 shared destroyed, 4 destroyed and 1 shared and 8 destroyed respectively. Harries was killed in a post-war flying accident and West died in a Spitfire in 1943. Only Chris Doll would survive his career as an RAF fighter pilot (*Chris Doll*)

about 85 mph and ran into the thick mist straight away. It had rained heavily earlier that morning, and I couldn't know that I was heading for a very muddy patch. The wheels hit the mud, dug themselves in and the Hurricane went onto its nose and straight over onto its back. I was now upside down, arms flung out to each side of the cockpit, and gradually my head and face, which was covered with helmet, goggles and mask, were pushed into the mud. It was like being upside down on a cross and unable to breathe. Suddenly, I felt a trickle of warm liquid running down my stomach and onto my chest. In a flash, my mind went back to that Alsatian. I knew then that I was dying. And I died.

'Somehow or other, the groundcrew lifted up one wing and lifted me out of the cockpit. As I came to, I saw three ambulance men in white and realised I had died and gone to heaven. As I gazed at them I said "So it is true. There is another life and there are angels". It took them a long while to convince me otherwise! Thinking about it afterwards, I had to admit that these three hulking ambulance men were hardly that angelic!

'I also owed my life to an inexcusable error of airmanship in that I had forgotten to raise my Hurricane seat for better landing vision. I never failed to do this in my entire flying career – except this time. Had I done so my neck would have been broken. So, the angels were with me even if I weren't with them yet!'

Unfortunately, the official Air Ministry view of Chris Doll's mishap was somewhat different, stating it to be an 'error of judgment' due to the pilot overshooting and overturning on the 'rough' at the end of the runway. It is difficult, if not impossible, to see how the unfortunate Plt Off Doll could have foreseen the muddy patch lurking in the mist, or how he could have done anything other than land in the one mist-free bit of aerodrome that he could see! The vagaries of Air Force life were, however, sometimes inexplicable, unfair and unforgiving, but thankfully Doll was not disciplined for what seems to have been an unavoidable accident.

Towards the end of the month heavy snowfall, so reminiscent of the previous winter, closed down all flying at Drem and Turnhouse, leaving a gap in the UK's air defences. To close that gap, efforts were made to temporarily clear Drem's runway of snow and fly across to the Fleet Air Station at Crail – HMS *Jackdaw* – which was still operational. Ultimately, 12 aircraft and pilots made the hop to Crail, where No 43 Sqn stayed until 1 March, when a return to a newly thawed-out Drem was effected.

Toward the end of the month, on the 24th, Plt Off West managed to make a good forced landing near Drone Hill in P2436 when the engine failed as he forgot to switch over from the reserve to main tank. Otherwise, there was little of any great significance to report for the month, save for the endless round of under training pilots in and out, patrols, practice formation flying, aerobatics, local flying, air firing and the like. It was the same old story in April, although during the course of the month the unit began to re-equip with the Hurricane II. It was not until May that things started to warm up, both metaphorically as well as meteorologically.

On the night of 5/6 May Sqn Ldr Dalton-Morgan began a run of squadron 'kills' which saw his personal tally rise by six and one shared victories by the beginning of October. His successes also re-established No 43 Sqn's standing as a unit with teeth (or should that be claws and spurs?), albeit that their sojourn continued in the relatively quiet No 13 Group. This fresh spate of kills at least did a little to assuage the pilots' thirst to get back to the south, where they had been watching with envy as fighter squadrons there moved into a more offensive role. Dalton-Morgan's first kill that night was a Ju 88, sent like a fiery comet into the sea off Anstruther. On a second patrol several hours later he sent another unidentified enemy aircraft down into the water off Fifeness.

The following night Sqn Ldr Dalton-Morgan got another Ju 88, which was seen to fall into the sea at 0155 hrs by the Observer Corps post at St Abbs Head. The unit, though, lost its first Hurricane Mk II that night when Sgt A H Hayley, an Australian, became lost whilst returning from a patrol over Glasgow at 0300 hrs. Hayley did not call early enough for a direction finding fix, and when he did so he was out of range. Short of fuel, and way off to the south, Sgt Hayley eventually baled out of Z2801 near Barnard Castle.

During the following afternoon, and whilst engaged on a training flight, Flt Lt du Vivier and Plt Off Mize, an American, were ordered to intercept a Ju 88. They duly shared in the destruction of this raider, which was also sent into the sea, but not before the gunner had scored hits on du Vivier's Hurricane in several places.

Perhaps still flushed with his first taste of action, and his half-kill, Mize was involved in a tragic landing accident at Acklington (which he was using as a base during aerial gunnery training) the very next day when he ran into a civilian worker on the edge of the runway. Sadly, the man was killed outright and manslaughter charges were preferred against the unfortunate American. Mize was shaken, but unhurt, and Hurricane Z2638 only slightly damaged, although it is notable that Mize was flying again that very night in Z2685. At the subsequent inquest the American pilot was exonerated of all blame, although by then he had already completed his training on No 43 Sqn and had been posted out to another operational unit on 9 May 1941.

Another American, Plt Off Scudday, was involved in a further incident on 8 May when he experienced engine trouble and force landed on the airfield, wheels up flaps down, causing serious damage to Z2684.

On the 10th, over the Pentland Hills, Flt Lt du Vivier and Plt Off Hutchinson intercepted and chased to Berwick-upon-Tweed a solitary Ju 88. Both pilots opened fire, and claimed the aircraft as damaged although reliable witnesses later watched the enemy aircraft falling into the sea a long way out after the crew had been seen to parachute down. Du Vivier was flying Z3079 and Hutchinson Z2638, newly repaired after sustaining minor damage in Mize's accident of the 8th.

After the *Bismarck* action at the end of May, HMS *Prince of Wales,* damaged in that action, made its way back to Scapa Flow. To cover against any potential Luftwaffe threat, No 43 Sqn made a temporary detached move to Prestwick (Ayr), and it was from here on the 28th that Red Section, comprising Flt Lt du Vivier (Z3031) and Plt Off Czajkowski (Polish), were scrambled to intercept a lone Ju 88. The pair sighted the Junkers at 24,000 ft, flying east, just south of Glasgow shortly before 1430 hrs. Unfortunately, Czajkowski's engine developed an oil leak as they were about to engage. Breaking off, he force landed on an airfield under construction at Longtown, causing slight damage to his Hurricane due to the state of the runway.

Pressing on alone, du Vivier caught up with the bomber and carried out three attacks, pieces falling off the Junkers under a withering and accurate hail of fire. Burning, the Ju 88 crashed at Boghall Hill, Newcastleton, with two dead crew on board – the other two had baled out and were made PoWs. The aircraft (Wk-Nr 0615 VB+KM) was from 2./*Aufklarungsgruppe* Ob.d.L., and it had taken off from Brest at 1000 hrs that day with orders to photograph Glasgow. The observer, Leutnant Fritz Gortam, and the flight engineer Gefreiter Heinrich Matthias, were the two fatalities. The pilot was Gefreiter Herbert Niepel and his radio operator/gunner Gefreiter Josef Lindorfer.

In the bomber's final moments it was Lindorfer who put hits into du Vivier's oil tank, causing him to land at Acklington. All of the unit's other recent claims had fallen over water, and this burnt out wreck on land presented an opportunity for squadron personnel to visit and view their prize.

The unfortunate Czajkowski, having missed a share of the Newcastleton Ju 88, was doubtless hoping for another slice of action when on patrol again with du Vivier on 2 June. This time, again in Hurricane Z2638, returning from an operational patrol he went into a sharp turn at 600 ft over wooded countryside to the north of Berwick, stalled and crashed into a field. Badly injured, he was taken to a military hospital in Edinburgh.

On the 8th it was again the turn of Sqn Ldr Dalton-Morgan to make a claim. This time, and again at night, he at first spotted the shadow of a Ju 88 flicking across the moonlit sea (perhaps a wholly unique method of interception?) 15 miles off St Abbs Head. Diving down from 2000 ft, Dalton-Morgan closed to within 75 yards of the aircraft that he had found flying a mere 100 ft above the sea and opened fire. After the second burst the enemy aircraft hit the water and broke up.

At about this time, word came through that the badly burned Flt Sgt Ottewill, injured on 7 June 1940 over France, had now been released from hospital, and with his release came word from HQ Fighter Command that his claim of one Bf 109 destroyed during that action had finally been allowed. So much had happened in the life of the squadron during the preceding 12 months that the actions of a year ago must have seemed like ancient history to those few still with the unit whose knowledge went that far back!

On 11 July the CO again managed yet another night 'kill'. Taking off at 0015 hrs to investigate an 'X' raid, he found two He 111s attacking a convoy 20 miles east of Bell Rock. One of them, flying at 200 ft and making a run-in to bomb the vessels, was attacked from dead astern by Dalton-Morgan at very close range. Almost at once, and without any avoiding action or return fire, the Heinkel dived straight into the sea. The claim was confirmed by the ships, and Dalton-Morgan reasonably concluded that the Heinkel crew had been so intent on their attack on the shipping that they had not seen their own attacker.

On the 21st of the month – appropriately Belgian Independence Day – Leroy du Vivier was invested with the Croix de Guerre by the exiled Belgian prime minister in London. No award could surely have been better earned, or more richly deserved.

On 24 July Sqn Ldr Dalton-Morgan took a half share in another Ju 88, although what started as a practice interception flight turned into the real thing and became something of an exciting, if not harrowing, adventure! Unlike his previous six kills, this was not at night, and the story is best told, verbatim, from the No 43 Sqn Operational Record Book;

'Blue Section, Sqn Ldr Dalton-Morgan and Plt Off Bourne, took off on a practice interception flight and after 25 minutes, east of May Island, sighted a Ju 88 at sea level. The enemy aircraft turned due east and a tail chase took place at over 300 mph for about three miles. When 1000 yards away Blue 1 (Dalton-Morgan) developed engine trouble and white smoke

This was Sqn Ldr Dalton-Morgan's Hurricane, and it was photographed at Drem in 1941 along with the flight sergeant in charge of 'B' Flight, Flt Sgt Savage. It was Savage who had been involved in the Sgt Hallowes 'episode' on 20 July 1940! The Hurricane in this photograph, apart from the colourful fighting cock emblem, has a red back plate to the sky spinner (*Chris Doll*)

filled his cockpit. In spite of this he kept going and closed on the enemy aircraft, which opened fire at 600 yards without hitting him. After the first attack from the port quarter, the condition of Blue 1's engine got worse, but he closed the distance and delivered, in all, three attacks. After the starboard engine slowed up, Blue 2 continued the attacks from the starboard quarter, and his shots were seen to enter the wing and fuselage. The Ju 88 crashed into the sea.

'By this time Blue 1's engine had stopped, and he force-landed the Hurricane (Z3143) in the sea, tail first, with flaps and undercarriage up. He was picked up in his rubber dinghy 1 hour 45 minutes later by HMS *Ludlow* and transferred to a trawler, which landed him at Aberdeen from where he was taken to RN Hospital Kingseat. In the impact with the water the gunsight had pushed his front teeth into his palate and he had also suffered from exposure. Plt Off Bourne had circled the crash scene to get a fix and Flt Lt du Vivier then arrived to take over, circling the dinghy and attracting the attention of HMS *Ludlow*. Du Vivier assumed command of the squadron from this date.'

Dalton-Morgan was discharged from hospital on 1 August and granted a well-earned 28-day leave. Meanwhile, the OC RAF Drem, Wg Cdr Eeles, was moved to write the following eulogy of the Welshman's actions;

'I consider this to be a classical example of how a first class pilot can attack an enemy aircraft when his engine is failing, shoot it down, force land in the sea and get away with it.'

At the end of July, Lt Birksted and 2nd Lt Berg of the Royal Norwegian Air Force joined the squadron, bringing to a total of 16 the number of different nationalities the squadron had had on its strength. Pilots from England, Scotland, Ireland, Wales, Australia, New Zealand, South Africa,

The CO of No 43 Sqn, Sqn Ldr Roy du Vivier, is pictured in full flying kit at around the time of the Dieppe operation. The Hurricane in the blast pen is FT-F, serial number unknown

Recently promoted Sqn Ldr du Vivier perches on the cockpit edge of Hurricane IIC *URUNDI* during the early spring of 1942. Note the ribbon for the Belgian's DFC below his wings, this award having been presented to him just a matter of weeks earlier. Du Vivier had seen action against the Germans in CR.42 and Firefly biplanes in May 1940, before fleeing to England and joining the RAF. Briefly returning to the Belgian air force post-war, du Vivier worked for Shell Aviation and then Sabena in New York, where he was killed in a motorcycling accident on 2 September 1981

Canada, India, Poland, Czechoslovakia, France, Belgium, USA and Norway had all served time with the 'Fighting Cocks'. Of the Americans, a number of published sources state that future ace Col James Goodson, later of the USAAF's 4th Fighter Group, served at some time on No 43 Sqn. None of the official records examined bear this out, and it is the author's belief that Goodson never served with the unit.

August proved to be an action-free if not an accident free month. On the 20th, when ferrying one of the old Hurricane Is (V6537 FT-E) back to the squadron after repair, a Flg Off Eyskens crashed at RAF Henlow when he retracted the undercarriage before getting airborne. Repaired again by the 23rd, V6537 seems not to have again returned to No 43 Sqn, instead the war-weary airframe going to No 13 MU. It was also on the 23rd that Plt Off Bourne, during practice attacks on the squadron Magister, found that the flaps of Hurricane Z2908 had jammed down at 15 degrees. After trying for an hour to free them, he force landed at Drem, damaging the aircraft – the squadron ORB shows this to have been on 23 August, although the AM Form 78 Accident Record Card gives 21 August as the date! The month drew to a close with American Plt Off M S Vosberg suffering a glycol leak and engine failure in Z2388, and having to force land south of Middleton (another discrepancy here in that the ORB gives the serial as Z2388 and the AM Form 78 shows Z2629!).

September, as with August, provided no action against the enemy, but instead witnessed the ever depressing round of flying accidents. On the 1st

Sgt J W Welling was killed in a night flying accident. A pilot under training, he had successfully completed his dusk and night landings and night flying, and was now assigned to do a night patrol. Taking off at 2140 hrs, Welling reported being airborne shortly afterwards, and then nothing more was heard from him until his aircraft was seen to crash in the River Tay, west of the Tay Bridge, at 2200 hrs. The weather was good, and it was a bright moonlit night, and it was presumed that he lost control for some unknown reason and spun in. Welling's body was recovered the next morning and sent for burial at his home in Old Windsor.

On the 5th yet another accident claimed the life of Plt Off David Bourne when he crashed near Donibristle in Z2971. As Black 1, he took off with Plt Off Mehta (Black 2) at 0845 hrs. Flying over low cloud at approximately 1000 ft north of Firth, Bourne made a steep turn onto a new vector, lost control and spun into a wooded hillside. The Hurricane caught fire on impact and was burnt out. Bourne had joined No 43 Sqn as a Section Leader under training, and was showing great promise.

Perhaps, at this point, and having regard to the high number of flying accidents on the squadron recorded in the preceding paragraphs, it is worth reminding the reader that this was a unit then charged with finishing the training of pilots fresh out of OTUs. As such, these were by definition inexperienced aviators being pushed and tested to the absolute limit in high performance aeroplanes before posting on to frontline squadrons. Inevitably, then, a fairly high percentage of flying accidents would be expected to occur. Sadly, many were fatal.

Another squadron detachment to RAF Valley, in north Wales, took place from 10 to 17 September so as to allow No 43 Sqn to carry out convoy patrols, as well as providing cover in that sector of No 12 Group left exposed by the interchange of squadrons. A series of patrols were flown without accident or incident, although maintaining serviceability proved to be a challenge with the squadron infrastructure remaining at Drem.

Plt Off Freddie Lister holds up an emblem 'borrowed' from an Edinburgh nightclub alongside one of the squadron's Hurricanes while other pilots look on at Drem in early 1942. These men are, from left to right, Sgt Ball, Plt Off Daniels, Sqn Ldr du Vivier and Flt Lts Hutchison and May

Shortly after returning to Scotland, news reached No 43 Sqn about a move south to Acklington, and as preparations were made to depart Drem Sqn Ldr Dalton-Morgan journeyed to London, and Buckingham Palace, to receive a Bar to his DFC. On the 28th came a welcome visitor to Drem in the form of No 43 Sqn's ex-commanding officer Wg Cdr George Lott DSO DFC, who had now been posted to No 13 Group as station commander at Acklington, No 43's new home. Lott had lost his operational flying category, but was still cleared to fly single- and twin-engined aeroplanes. All the same, a brief flight by Lott in No 43 Sqn's Magister (V1101) at Drem saw Plt Off Hutchison tag along as safety pilot.

The 'Fighting Cock's' swansong at Drem saw none other than Sqn Ldr Dalton-Morgan making yet another night kill. On 2 October he took off for a patrol at 2115 hrs, and hearing that an air raid was in progress on Newcastle, he saw bombs bursting way off to the south. Heading full-speed at 10,000 ft for a point 20 miles south-east of the Farne Islands, where he estimated he would intercept raiders either approaching or leaving Newcastle, Dalton-Morgan saw a twin-engined aircraft flying northwards at around 8000 ft some 1000 ft off his starboard beam. Turning and diving below the aircraft, and coming up from dead astern, he identified the machine as a Ju 88 and carried out three attacks from above and astern. After the first attack there was return fire, but the Junkers then burst into flames, dived steeply and crashed into the sea. Plt Off Hutchison witnessed the aircraft crash, thus confirming the claim.

On 4 October 1941 the entire paraphernalia of an operational squadron was relocated to Acklington, a station not unfamiliar to a few old hands on No 43. The unit had spent longer at Drem than any other base since September 1939, and whilst there the 'Fighting Cocks' had claimed 11 enemy aircraft destroyed ($6^1/2$ of these were credited to Sqn Ldr Dalton-Morgan) and had three pilots killed in accidents. More importantly, it had trained no less than 86 pilots, ten of whom were still with the squadron. These were pilots who had been hand-picked and creamed off by the CO and flight commanders, who all had an eye for promising talent. Amongst them was Sgt 'Joe' Pipa, who had been the reliable and steady No 2 to Sqn Ldr Dalton-Morgan for much of 1941.

The primary reason behind No 43 Sqn moving to Acklington was to allow its pilots to work up operational tactics with No 1460 Flt, an experimental unit equipped with Turbinlite Havocs. The idea was that No 43 Sqn would supply fighters as a foil to the flight's flying searchlight role, although the whole Turbinlite project proved to be a failure. Certainly, No 43 Sqn gained some useful nightfighting experience, but this counted for nought when the project was abandoned following a large number of co-operation flights, all of which ended without success.

No 43 Sqn had barely settled into Acklington when the depressing routine of flying accidents commenced. On 12 October Flt Lt Hutchison (Z3270) and Sgt J A R Turner (Z2807), a Canadian, were carrying out practice combat attacks near Alnwick. Hutchison was the target, and Turner made a dummy attack and came up from beneath him. As he did so, the propeller of Z3270 sliced off the tail of Z2807, sending the latter spinning down out of control and killing Turner when it crashed. Hutchison lost consciousness but regained control and carried out a forced landing near Embleton, with cuts and bruises on his face, no propeller

**Left and below**
Sgt Josef Pipa of Czechoslovakia joined No 43 Sqn at Usworth in October 1940, and went on to serve with the unit for some considerable period of time. He became a reliable and steady pilot, regularly flying as No 2 to his CO, Sqn Ldr Tom Dalton-Morgan. On 9 December 1941, whilst flying Hurricane IIC BD734 FT-O, Pipa claimed a half share in a Ju 88 with his flight commander, Flt Lt May (in BD715 FT-M). The bomber was sent crashing into the sea off Seaham Harbour with one engine engulfed in flames

blades and no working instruments. Later that same day Sgt J G Meredith made an error of judgment landing Z2577 and hit a recessed flare path, causing the undercarriage to collapse. It had been a bad day.

To compound the gloom, No 43 Sqn suffered a morale shaking blow on 3 November when Indian pilot Plt Off Hukam Chaud Mehta was killed in a flying accident. Mehta was a hugely popular figure on the squadron, and his loss was felt all the more keenly. He had been with the unit some five months, was considered to be a very good pilot, and had been developing into a fine Section Leader. Flying Z3150 (the aeroplane in which Sqn Ldr Dalton-Morgan had claimed two kills on 5/6 May), he had run into bad weather and asked for a homing. Receiving and flying on the last heading given to him, he was flown straight into the side of Peel Fell. In a sad ceremony at Newcastle conducted by N K Roy, the Indian High Commissioner, Mehta was cremated in accordance with Hindu rites.

On the 14th, over a particularly cold and forbidding North Sea, Sgt C G S Williams, an Australian, experienced engine failure and ditched ten miles east of Blyth in Hurricane Z2968. As he scrambled out of his sinking fighter, he lost his one-man 'K' type dinghy, but as his No 2, Sgt Pipa, circled above, he realised his friend's predicament, pulled out his own dinghy from under his parachute, inflated it, and successfully dropped it to Williams. Continuing to circle, Pipa obtained a fix and called for an ASR launch, which eventually plucked the pilot from the water. Williams was admitted to the Thomas Knight Hospital with severe shock, a deep cut in his leg and a cut eyelid, but thanks to Pipa he was still alive.

Returning to Acklington, Pipa told nobody about the dinghy episode, and it was only discovered when Williams later told the story. For this feat Pipa was awarded a Bar to his Czech War Cross. This is another example where official records do not agree on the date. The ORB gives 14 November, whilst the AM Form 78 states the 19th, which is also the date given in the Log Book of another squadron pilot, Flt Lt Freddie Lister. However, the sequence of entries in the ORB would tend to indicate that the 14th is the correct date, unless the entry was made up some time later based upon unreliable contemporaneous notes.

As the year drew to an end there was the almost inevitable flying accident when Plt Off Malarowski crashed in the Firth of Forth following engine failure in R4227 during a standing patrol on 15 December. Fortunately, the Polish pilot was plucked from the water unharmed by a Royal Navy destroyer and taken to Scapa.

A New Year was just around the corner. It would bring pastures new, with fresh challenges and excitement.

## SOUTH AGAIN

Although it would be yet some while before the move south took place, many of the events over the coming weeks and months led those on the squadron to suspect that something was in the offing. For one thing, the numbers of under training pilots arriving directly from the OTU had declined, and there appeared to be a move to stabilise No 43 Sqn's establishment with combat-ready pilots.

The tempo and type of training undertaken by squadron pilots also changed markedly, although for some months the co-operation with the Turbinlite Havocs of No 1460 Flt continued without any form of success. In fact, there is almost a note of relief in the squadron ORB which recorded that for the month of February the bad weather had presented little opportunity to conduct co-operation with No 1460 Flt.

January, too, had been a fairly quiet month, although Sgt H R Lea and Flt Sgt C G S Williams had both been involved in relatively minor flying accidents. Most notably, though, Sqn Ldr Dalton-Morgan had been posted away to perform fighter controller's duties with No 13 Group. His replacement was the newly-promoted Sqn Ldr Leroy du Vivier, who duly became the first Belgian to command a RAF fighter squadron.

During March No 43 Sqn was selected to carry out service trials with the Franks Suit, which was designed to prevent pilots blacking out during high G manoeuvres. In effect, this was the forerunner of the modern fast jet pilot's G-Suit. The squadron was also chosen to trial new Rotol Jablo Sandwich propeller blades, these being fitted to eight of No 43's Hurricane IICs. The only other item of particular note recorded in the squadron diary for the month was that Sgt Le Gal (Free French) was promoted to the rank of sergent chef (flight sergeant) with effect from 15 March. Le Gal had shown great promise, and had also distinguished himself under training at his OTU, where he had saved his Hurricane during an in-flight engine fire, and been awarded the comparatively rare AFM (this was possibly the only award of the Air Force Medal to a French national).

The month of April was marred by the death of American Flt Sgt H J Helbock on the 5th, who was killed in Hurricane Z2983 while testing the Franks Suit. Performing a high speed stall too near to the ground, the Hurricane crashed at South Side Farm, Belford. The subsequent enquiry found that Helbock had disobeyed orders, which were to avoid all violent manoeuvres below 10,000 ft. Whether the Franks Suit had been a contributory factor in the accident, or whether it had served in giving Helbock undue confidence, is not clear. However, the ORB for the end of April noted that No 43 Sqn's tests on the Franks Suit were still ongoing.

On 17 April, during what were now becoming regular low-level training flights, Flt Sgt A J Reed of Canada was killed when his aircraft, Z3068, struck roadside electricity cables at Whittingham, Northumberland, and crashed. The pilot had been engaged with the Army on Exercise *Oatmeal*, and although he was noted as a keen and sensible pilot, it is recorded that he had been led too low by his section leader.

The month ended on a brighter note, however. On the 25th, Sqn Ldr du Vivier (BN230), Plt Off Daniels (BN954) and Sgt Wik (BD715) were patrolling at 32,000 ft when they saw a Ju 88 3000 ft below them. It immediately opened fire on the Hurricanes as they approached and began to dive. The Hurricanes found it impossible to close to less than 400 yards, but opened fire nevertheless. Du Vivier's Hurricane was hit by a bullet that entered the cockpit and went through his Mae West without hitting him, but caused splinter wounds in his face and neck. The Ju 88 was then seen to crash into the sea off Newcastle and explode after one member of the crew baled out. Three burning patches were left on the water.

On 1 May the well respected Frenchman, Le Gal, on an 'X' raid interception at 0730 hrs, ran short of fuel in Z3316 and was unable to get into Catterick due to low cloud. In attempting a forced landing, Le Gal tried to bounce over a low wall and crashed, but was unhurt. The next day he and his French companion, Flt Sgt Buiron, were posted out to No 87 Sqn.

'A' Flight No 43 Sqn relax whilst at readiness at Acklington in May 1942. At the window is American John Daniels, whilst sprawling in the chairs are Frenchman Sgt Buiron, Canadian Jackie Reed and New Zealanders Maury Smith and Wilf Webster

Once a No 43 Sqn Hurricane, this tangled heap of wreckage is all that remains of P5197 after Sgt J Lewis had been forced to bale out of it on 16 May 1942 at 1615 hrs following a glycol leak during formation practice

Two more accidents marred the rest of May, with Sgt J Lewis in Z5197 suffering a glycol leak and being forced to bale out during formation practice on the 16th. His aircraft crashed near Chathill. At 0015 hrs on the 20th, Flt Lt A B Hutchison was killed in BD954 when he crashed whilst orbiting to await a co-operating Havoc. He had reported difficulty with his undercarriage and is thought to have had his head down in the cockpit when he entered cloud, stalled and spun in. The Hurricane burst into flames on impact and Hutchison was killed instantly.

Brighter news, however, reached No 43 Sqn on the 23rd when seven aircraft and groundcrew were attached to RAF Ford in No 11 Group for temporary duty. Thirteen pilots made the trip, and two new Hurricanes were delivered to the unit at Ford from No 19 MU. A rather fed-up Flt Lt Freddie Lister remained behind at Acklington with four Hurricanes to continue practice trips with the Havocs. It was with some relief that he welcomed the squadron's return to base on 31st after they had completed a whole week of authorised low flying and co-operation work with the Army. Something, the pilots adjudged, was very much afoot!

Indeed it was, and on 16 June the unit bade adieu to Acklington and moved back to its old home at Tangmere. In all, 14 aircraft on the current squadron strength made the journey, and with one party of essential groundcrew proceeding by air, the remainder came later by train. There followed, from 16 until 30 June, intensive training in the strafing of ground targets and formation flying – the latter mostly at low level. During that period only one operational flight was undertaken.

The latter mission took place on the 28th when, at 0445 hrs, Red, Green and Blue sections of four aircraft each, led by Sqn Ldr du Vivier, (BN230) Flt Lt Lister (Z2915) and Flt Lt Armstrong (HL562), respectively, took off

to search for enemy minesweepers off the French coast. They crossed out over Selsey Bill at 500 ft and flew straight toward Le Havre. When ten miles from the French coast two destroyers were spotted but not attacked, although the vessels opened up an intense barrage of anti-aircraft fire. The Hurricanes then turned to starboard and returned, there being no sign of the minesweepers. Landfall was made at St Catherines Point and all aircraft landed safely at 0600 hrs. For the first time squadron pilots felt that they were beginning to take the war to the enemy, and there would certainly be more of the same yet to come.

In July No 43 Sqn took on the intruding duties of No 1 Sqn (which had moved to Acklington to re-equip with Typhoons), along with the allied roles of searchlight and Havoc-Turbinlite co-operation – the latter now with No 1455 Flt. As the ORB put it, 'A new phase of squadron history commenced'. It was ordered that aircraft were to be available each night, with five allocated to Intruder work, four for Havoc co-operation and four for searchlight co-operation. To reflect this new role, the squadron Hurricanes were finished in a mix of day fighter camouflage scheme and

These line up shots of No 43 Sqn's Hurricane IIs at Tangmere in August 1942 are interesting in that they show the two camouflage schemes in use on the squadron at the same time – the temperate day fighter scheme (foreground) and the night black Intruder scheme in the distance. The first aircraft is Z3684 FT-L, flown by Plt Off R Barker during the Dieppe operation. Further down the line is BP703 FT-O in which Plt Off Snell was shot down over Dieppe (*IWM*)

night intruder black overall. On the 11th of the month, Flt Sgt Edwards (South African), who had been with the squadron since March, took off on a practice flight at 1745 hrs and failed to return. He became the first No 43 Sqn casualty of this spell at Tangmere.

During the month, though, at least 30 Intruder sorties were flown over France, but with limited success. Typical was the mission of the 31st, conducted by Australian Sgt G Ball in Z3895 between 0135 and 0410 hrs. The official report states, 'Target Evreux and St Andre. Arrived in target area 0225 hrs and patrolled for one hour between 1000 and 12,000 ft. No activity, so disabled engine of a goods train west north-west of Evreux, making three two-second attacks. Many strikes seen. Train stopped with a jerk after the first burst and was left enveloped in steam'.

Earlier though, on the 26th, New Zealander Sgt R F Whitten in HL863 FT-T had failed to return from an Intruder sortie to the Fecamp area. He was buried at Le Havre. Stooging around France, looking for returning German bombers or shooting up the occasional train was not always without cost.

The ORB records at the end of July that a number of squadron aircraft were marked up with names, five of those being given as *Kiuu, Itaga,*

Sgt 'Al' Lynds of Canada was one of No 43 Sqn's Night Intruder pilots, and he was killed on just such a mission over France in BN229 FT-D on 5 August 1942

*Rabora, Mahenge* and *Asosa*. Unfortunately, the squadron adjutant failed to note which name was applied to which Hurricane!

Into August, and there was a further No 43 Sqn loss on an Intruder sortie. This time Sgt A G 'Al' Lynds of Canada failed to come home from a sortie to Evreux in BN229 FT-D on the 5th and now lies buried in Pont Audembert cemetery.

The Intruder operations and Havoc co-operation flights continued unabated, but a sense of urgency with the stockpiling of essential stores, ammunition and long range tanks, and the achievement of high levels of serviceability, told of a bigger story yet to unfold.

On the 15th, a visit to No 43 Sqn by Air Chief Marshal Sir Sholto Douglas heightened the anticipation – as did the order on the 16th to maintain all aircraft at a state of '60 minutes available'. No flying took place on the 17th or 18th and all leave was cancelled, mail was stopped, and all ranks confined to camp. Before dawn on the 19th all members of the

American Plt Off J Daniels poses in the cockpit of a night intruder Hurricane IIC at Tangmere in August 1942. The significance of the name *R. P. DE DEKEN* remains unknown, although it was almost certainly the name of the donor of this presentation Hurricane. The photograph cannot be tied to any identifiable No 43 Sqn serial number and thus the history of this particular aeroplane remains uncertain. The heavy weathering of the night black finish is noticeable in this photograph. Daniels, having completed a tour of duty with No 43 Sqn, was transferred to the USAAF and later shot down and made a PoW whilst flying with a P-39 unit in North Africa

squadron were roused and the pilots briefed as the aircraft were fuelled and armed. Operation *Jubilee*, the ill-fated commando raid on Dieppe, was underway, and No 43 Sqn was to play a major role.

Coming to readiness at 0400 hrs, the first mission of the day was flown by Sqn Ldr du Vivier (BN230), Flt Sgt H Wik (BD712), Sgt N Smith (Z3687), Sgt W Webster (Z3169), Flt Lt W Armstrong (HL562), Flt Sgt J D Lewis (AM315), Plt Off J Daniels (HL563), Plt Off J T Wills (HL560), Plt Off Trenchard-Smith (Z5153), Flt Lt F Lister (BN234), Plt Off A Snell (BP703) and Sgt G Ball (Z2915).

All 12 Hurricanes departed Tangmere at 0425 hrs, with orders to attack gun positions on the beaches and in the buildings immediately to the west of Dieppe harbour in order to suppress fire which was expected to come down on the commandos going ashore when No 43 Sqn arrived overhead. Now, the long hours spent low flying and practising attacks on ground targets made sense as that training came into its own.

One of those on the raid, Plt Off Ted Trenchard-Smith, wrote a detailed letter recounting the action to his mother in Australia, and as a contemporary account by one who was there, it provides an interesting historical insight into the actions of No 43 Sqn on that day through the eyes of one of its pilots;

'We were up at 0300 hrs, had breakfast and an hour-and-a-half later took off for Dieppe. By about 0500 hrs, with dawn just breaking, we were nearing the French coast and could see flashes of gunfire both from our ships and the Jerry shore batteries. From one side of the Channel to the other was a continuous convoy of ships. As we got into position to attack, the landing craft were almost up to the beaches. Now, the harbour and town came into sight, and we could see where bombers had dropped

Sqn Ldr du Vivier briefs pilots over a map at Acklington in 1942. They are, from left to right, Plt Off Lister, Sqn Ldr du Vivier, Flt Lts May and Hutchison (killed on 20 May 1942) and Plt Off Daniels

Sgt Tony Snell, photographed on Sqn Ldr du Vivier's Hurricane at Acklington (note the corner of du Vivier's personal emblem just above Snell's knee), also took part in the Dieppe operation. Flying Intruder black-painted Hurricane BP703 FT-O, his fighter was badly shot up and he baled out off Dieppe. Snell was rescued and returned to England. Subsequently commissioned, he went on to serve with No 43 Sqn in North Africa, but was eventually killed with the squadron when his Spitfire dived into the Mediterranean from high altitude on 31 August 1943 (*Chris Goss*)

bombs and smoke canisters on the cliffs to give us protection on the way out.

'As we dived into attack, there was a small amount of gunfire from the cliffs, and here and there fires had started, but everything looked moderately safe.

'Then, as though someone had pressed a button, every gun in Dieppe opened up – not only at us, but also at the vessels out at sea. I'll never forget what that barrage looked like as long as I live – and we had to go straight into it.

'I was flying Number 4 to the CO, and was on his left in the actual attack. My target was the left hand corner of the beach, the harbour entrance and surrounding buildings. Jerry was using tracer cannon shells and bullets, so on a conservative estimate of 30 guns firing 1000 rounds a minute, you can imagine what a sight it was. We were also using tracer.

'We went in at nought feet, pouring everything we could into the beach and promenade, then we were over the town, roof-hopping and flat out trying to dodge the flak. It was hopeless, and before we could reach the smoke cover, and in spite of the way I threw my kite around, in and out of streams of fire, I was hit just in front of the rudder by an explosive cannon shell which blew off half the fin and tore a huge hole in the tailplane. I was lucky, as I saw the lad in front of me ('Hank' Wik – author's note), who had been flying Number 2 to the CO, get hit in a bad way, and that was the last I saw of him. Almost at the same time a swarm of Fw 190s appeared from nowhere, and there were screams over the r/t from lads baling out or being hit. It was a ghastly sight – parachutes opening, aeroplanes diving into the ground and sea, and all the time this wall of coloured steel coming up with flashes and fires everywhere.

'Somehow or other I reached the smoke screen and felt marvellous flying in it, knowing that I could not be seen, and that I was going out to sea.

'By this time our squadron had broken up, and most of us were by ourselves. Although I'd been hit I still had full control (or thought I had!) and went in to make a second attack, rather foolishly, alone. I don't know why I did it, because I was properly shaken by now and sweating like a pig. I suppose it was because we had had it drummed into us how important this job was, and that we should make two runs – the first on the beaches and the second on the promenade buildings, hoping to wipe out gun positions in the windows and start fires with incendiary bullets.

'By now the landing craft were just about on the beach, and I flew over them so low that I could clearly see the men crouched on the decks. This time I emptied my guns into the windows and doors. I didn't see any

Plt Off Ted Trenchard-Smith was photographed beside his Hurricane IIC Z5153 FT-H at Tangmere in August 1942. Note the outline map of Australia and the jumping kangaroo on the cowling, indicative of the pilot's Antipodean roots! Trenchard-Smith brought this Hurricane back from Dieppe to Tangmere on 19 August 1942 with a very badly shot-up fuselage and tail

return fire, but once again had to go over the town and in through the same hell. It was rather unpleasant.

'When I tried to dive and turn the elevator control was very stiff and wouldn't react, making things uncomfortable. Actually, when I landed the groundcrew found that one of the control wires had been severed. The tail section just fell apart. There was also a bullet hole in my prop.

'Back at the airfield, the squadron landed in ones and twos. Only four aircraft were found to be without some sort of hole. We had lost one lad altogether, and another (Snell – author's note) bailed out near one of our ships and was picked up – he walked into the Mess that afternoon.'

Ted Trenchard-Smith's account makes for compelling and dramatic reading, and after his gruelling experience, and the frightening damage inflicted on his Hurricane, one would not have been surprised to find that he did not fly again that day. In fact, he flew three more sorties to Dieppe before the day was through.

Flt Sgt Wik, a Canadian, later turned up in a PoW camp and Plt Off Snell was rescued by the ASR service, while the remnants of No 43 Sqn

'Hank' Wik stands beside his CO's Hurricane at Acklington, immediately prior to the unit moving south to Tangmere. Note the crossed Belgian and RAF flags on the cockpit side above a No 43 Sqn chequerboard – du Vivier's personal emblem. The Canadian flight sergeant was shot down near Dieppe in BD712 FT-G and taken prisoner

landed back at Tangmere between 0600 and 0620 hrs. Hastily turned round, refuelled and rearmed, or replacement aircraft readied to fill the places of damaged Hurricanes, the squadron was off again by 0750 hrs for a second sortie – this time to search for ten E-boats coming out of Boulogne. Despite a long search nothing was found, and the unit was back by 0920 hrs.

The third sortie was flown at 1115 hrs, and this time No 43 Sqn was back over the beaches, where the flak was found to be much lighter. There were no losses this time, although several of the Hurricanes were hit. But this did not stop the squadron still having 12 Hurricanes available for the day's fourth, and last, mission at 1345 hrs.

Again, this was flown over the beaches, harbour and town in an attempt to silence at least six gun positions which had either not been hit or had been re-occupied. This time, Fw 190s bounced the Hurricanes, but only Sgt Bierer's Z2641 was hit. Notwithstanding the ever on-going debate about the wisdom, value and success of Operation *Jubilee*, it is a fact that No 43 Sqn had carried out the tasks allotted it with panache and determination. Repeatedly hosing the beach and town with deadly 20 mm cannon rounds, the dozens of Hurricane IICs tasked with providing fire suppression for *Jubilee* must have had an effect on the enemy.

That day, No 43 Sqn was the first RAF fighter unit over the beaches, and the 48 sorties it flew on 19 August 1942 was the highest number flown by the 21 squadrons in the Tangmere Sector. Flt Lt Lister, surviving a dramatic crash landing at Tangmere upon returning from the first sortie, flew on the remaining three missions, despite being badly shaken by his experiences. For his exploits that day he was awarded the DFC.

**Pilots of No 43 Sqn are seen in high spirits at Tangmere on 20 August 1942 – the day after the disastrous Dieppe operation. A squadron Hurricane forms the backdrop**

To all intents and purposes, Dieppe was the end of the No 43 Sqn story in England, and the unit now prepared for a temporary move to Kirton-in-Lindsey to ready for 'service overseas'. In the wake of *Jubilee* there was no squadron flying at Tangmere until 24 August, when Sgts Ball and Bierer resumed Intruder work, and again on the 27th when Intruder patrols were flown by Plt Off Wills and Sgt Ball. On the 28th the same pilots flew the final Havoc co-operation flights. It was the end of No 43 Sqn's operational flying in the United Kingdom during World War 2.

On 1 September the unit made the move northwards by air and train, taking with it all of the surviving Hurricanes to hand over to Nos 245 and 534 Sqns. On the 7th Sqn Ldr du Vivier, tour expired, relinquished command, handing over to Sqn Ldr Michael Rook, who was to lead the unit to its mystery overseas destination.

Meanwhile, squadron flying had all but ceased, although a few clapped-out ex-OTU Hurricane Is were made available, although these were rarely flown due to bad weather and unserviceability. If truth be known, it was probably a little beneath the dignity of No 43 Sqn's groundcrew to work on these ancient hand-me-downs, or even for the squadron pilots to want to fly them! A programme of packing, training, lectures and medical preparations got underway, and embarkation leave was granted to the entire squadron. Finally, on 26 October, a part contingent of No 43 Sqn, including the pilots, sailed from Greenock on the SS *Ashland* , the rest of the unit departing from there on the 28th aboard the SS *Strathmore*. The destination of both vessels remained unknown to the passengers.

A sea of pilots photographed around a No 43 Sqn Hurricane at Tangmere on 20 August 1942. In view of the large number of pilots brought together for this shot, it is likely that these include individuals from the other Tangmere-based Hurricane unit at this time, No 87 Sqn. Centre stage, however, is the CO of No 43 Sqn, Sqn Ldr du Vivier, who is holding aloft his cap

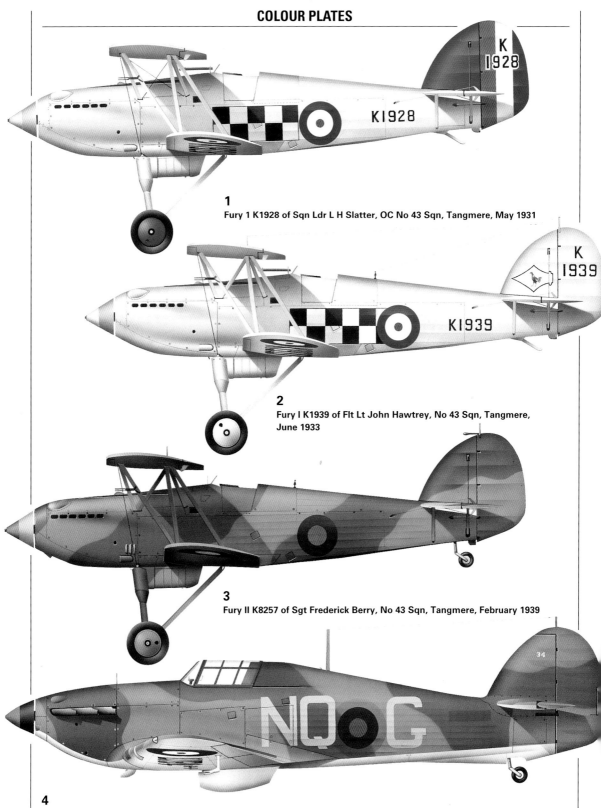

**1**
Fury 1 K1928 of Sqn Ldr L H Slatter, OC No 43 Sqn, Tangmere, May 1931

**2**
Fury I K1939 of Flt Lt John Hawtrey, No 43 Sqn, Tangmere,
June 1933

**3**
Fury II K8257 of Sgt Frederick Berry, No 43 Sqn, Tangmere, February 1939

**4**
Hurricane I L1734 of Plt Off John Kilmartin, No 43 Sqn, Tangmere, September 1939

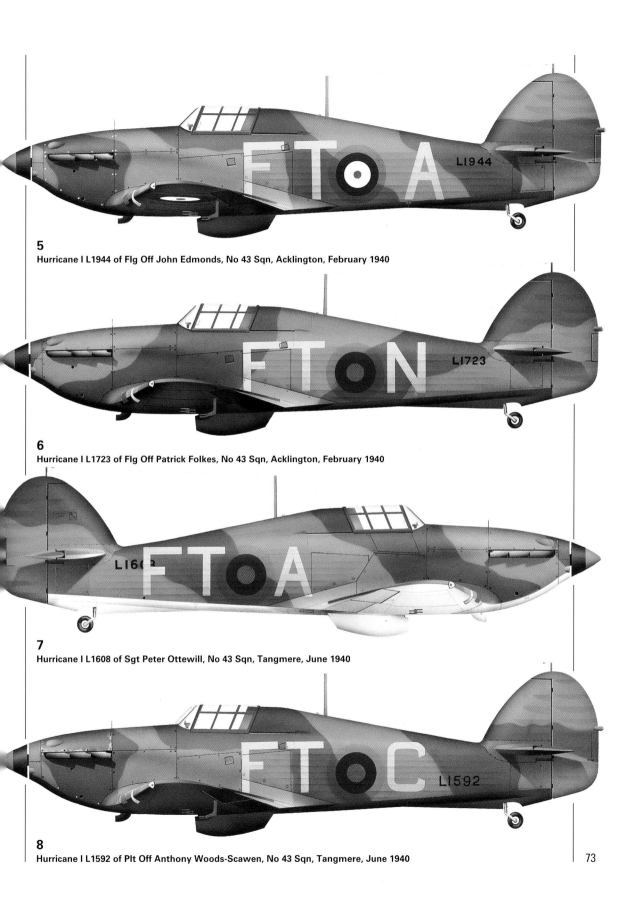

**5**
Hurricane I L1944 of Flg Off John Edmonds, No 43 Sqn, Acklington, February 1940

**6**
Hurricane I L1723 of Flg Off Patrick Folkes, No 43 Sqn, Acklington, February 1940

**7**
Hurricane I L1608 of Sgt Peter Ottewill, No 43 Sqn, Tangmere, June 1940

**8**
Hurricane I L1592 of Plt Off Anthony Woods-Scawen, No 43 Sqn, Tangmere, June 1940

**9**
Hurricane I L1847 of Sgt James Hallowes, No 43 Sqn, Acklington, February 1940

**10**
Hurricane I P3386 of Sgt Charles Hurry, No 43 Sqn, Tangmere, September 1940

**11**
Hurricane I P3784 of Sgt James Hallowes, No 43 Sqn, Tangmere, July 1940

**12**
Hurricane IIC BN230 of Sqn Ldr Leroy du Vivier, OC No 43 Sqn, Acklington, May 1942

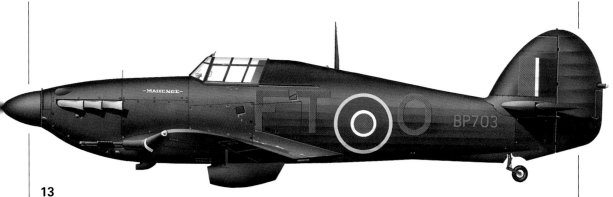

**13**
Hurricane IIC BP703 of Plt Off Anthony Snell, No 43 Sqn, Tangmere, August 1942

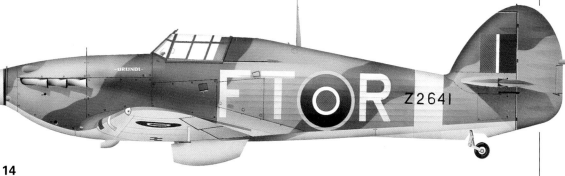

**14**
Hurricane IIB Z2641 of Sgt J Lewis, No 43 Sqn, Tangmere, August 1942

**15**
Hurricane IIC Z5153 of Plt Off Edward Trenchard-Smith, Tangmere, August 1942

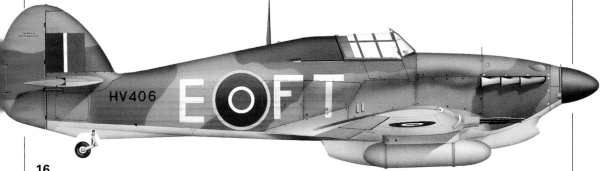

**16**
Hurricane IIC (tropicalised) HV406 of No 43 Sqn, Gibraltar, November 1942

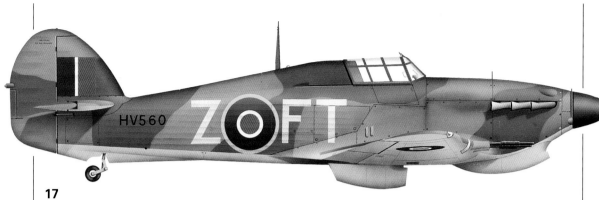

**17**
Hurricane IIC (tropicalised) HV560 of Sqn Ldr Michael Rook, OC No 43 Sqn, Maison Blanche, December 1942

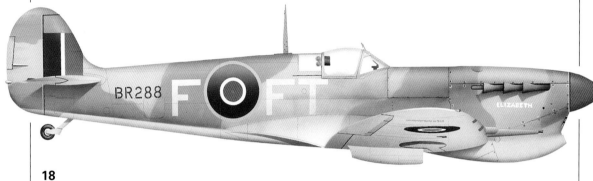

**18**
Spitfire VC (tropicalised) BR288 of Flt Lt Peter William Reading, No 43 Sqn, Hal Far, Malta, July 1943

**19**
Spitfire VC (tropicalised) ES352, No 43 Sqn, Pachino, Sicily, August 1943

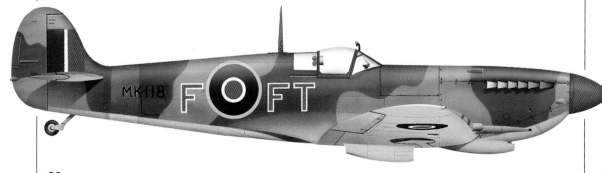

**20**
Spitfire IX MK118 of Plt Off Maurice Simpson, No 43 Sqn, Calvi, Corsica, August 1944

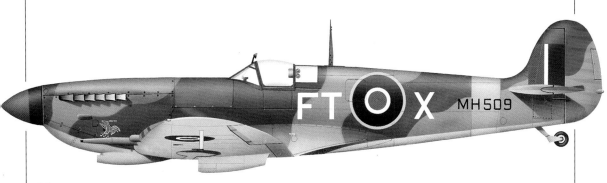

**21**
Spitfire IX MH509 of Wt Off J H Saville, No 43 Sqn, Grossetto, Italy, June 1944

**22**
Spitfire IX JL351 of Flt Sgt Williams, No 43 Sqn, Ravenna, Italy, April 1945

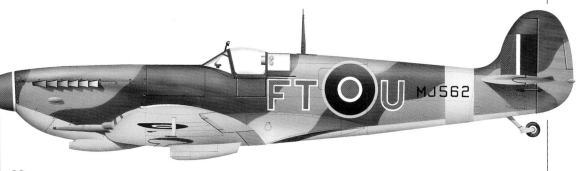

**23**
Spitfire IX MJ562 of Wt Off K F Hindson, No 43 Sqn, Campoformido, Italy, May 1945

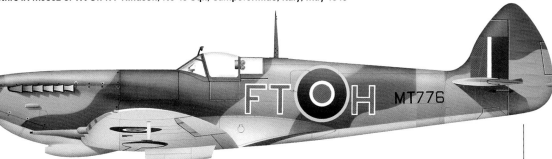

**24**
Spitfire VIII MT776 of Flt Lt B H Thomas, No 43 Sqn, Bron (Lyon), France, September 1944

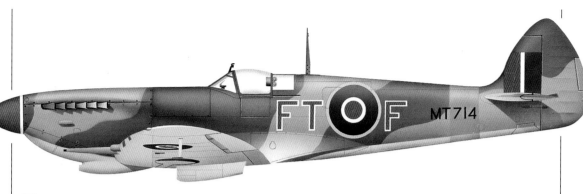

**25**
Spitfire VIII MT714 of Flt Lt A W Guest, No 43 Sqn, Ramatuelle, France, August 1944

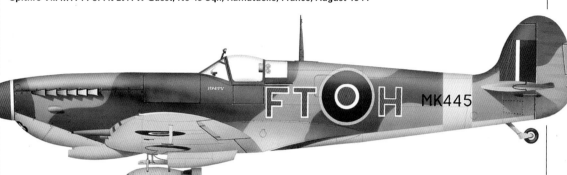

**26**
Spitfire IX MK445 of Flt Lt Peter Hedderwick, No 43 Sqn, Rimini, Italy, December 1944

**27**
Spitfire IX MK549 of Flt Lt Cecil Manson, No 43 Sqn, Ravenna, Italy, March 1945

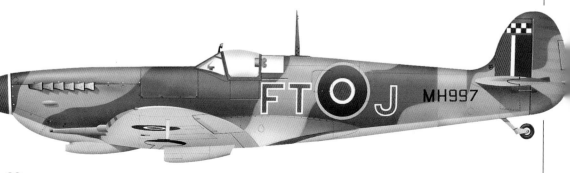

**28**
Spitfire IX MH997 of Lt Armstrong, No 43 Sqn, Campoformido, Italy, May 1945

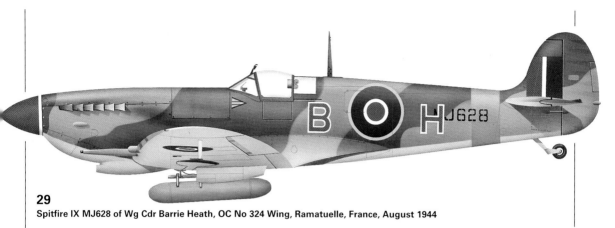

**29**
Spitfire IX MJ628 of Wg Cdr Barrie Heath, OC No 324 Wing, Ramatuelle, France, August 1944

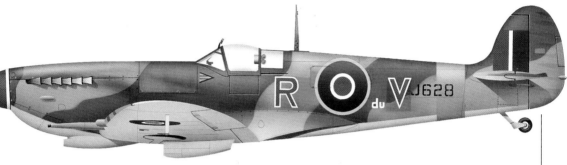

**30**
Spitfire IX MJ628 of Wg Cdr Leroy du Vivier, OC No 324 Wing, Nettuno (Anzio), Italy, May 1944

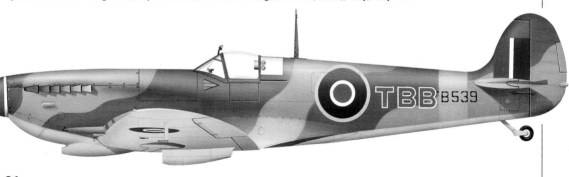

**31**
Spitfire IX TB539 of Wg Cdr T B Beresford, OC No 324 Wing, Klagenfurt, Austria, Summer 1945

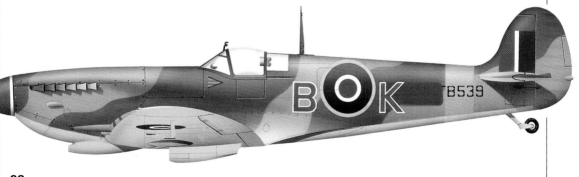

**32**
Spitfire IX TB539 of Wg Cdr Brian Kingcome, OC No 324 Wing, Zeltweg, Austria, Autumn 1945

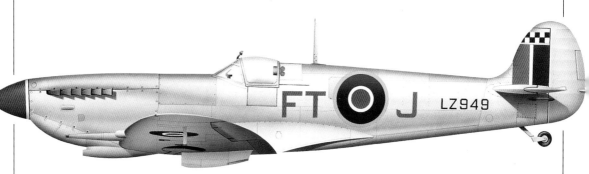

**33**
Spitfire IX LZ949 of No 43 Sqn, Klagenfurt, Austria, June 1945

Official crest of No 43 'Fighting Cocks' Sqn

# GIBRALTAR AND ONWARDS

O n 5 November the SS *Ashland* docked at Gibraltar and the pilots of No 43 Sqn disembarked for further instructions. Here, they were told that they would fly out from the 'Rock' at first light on the 8th and directly to Maison Blanche, in Algiers, to support the newly created second front in North Africa following the launching of Operation *Torch*. 'You will land' they were told 'regardless of whether Maison Blanche has been taken or not'. It all seemed a bit of a tall order, especially when the pilots were told, in a matter of fact way, that if the aerodrome had not been taken, and landing proved impossible, then they should simply bale out of their Hurricanes near some of our ships. At least, thought the pilots, the loss of the aeroplanes would be no great blow!

Having been shown a motley collection of tropicalised Hurricane IIs in the Gibraltar Aircraft Park, they were told to each select and test fly their own fighters. Having done so, all pilots were in agreement that the worn out OTU Hurricanes left behind at Kirton-in-Lindsey were infinitely better than the 'new' ones now on offer, in which they were now expected to make long over-water flights, and with a very uncertain destination.

However, accepting this order was made that much easier by the fact that they were briefed in Gibraltar by Wg Cdr John Simpson who had served on No 43 Sqn with distinction during France, Dunkirk and the Battle of Britain. For Simpson to have had to deliver such instructions to the unit must have been equally difficult. He understood what the pilots were thinking, and he, better than most, knew the risks that they were being asked to take. Was he sending No 43 Sqn off to certain destruction?

At 0800 hrs on 8 November two flights of nine Hurricanes each roared of from the 'Rock', one flight led by Sqn Ldr Rook and the other by Wg

On 8 November 1942 No 43 Sqn's new CO, Sqn Ldr Michael Rook, led 18 Hurricane IIC (Tropicalised) fighters off from Gibraltar to Maison Blanche, in Algeria, without even knowing if the airfield that they were heading for would be in friendly hands by the time they arrived! In the event it was, and Maison Blanche became the squadron's new home for some five months. In this photo, Sqn Ldr Rook is seen at the controls of HV406 FT-E (*RAFM*)

Cdr Michael Pedley. Also flying with them to Maison Blanche was Gp Capt Edwardes-Jones, commanding No 323 Wing, of which No 43 Sqn was now part. Simpson, with a lump in his throat, watched them all off.

Despite the decidedly second-rate nature of the squadron's new Hurricanes, all the aircraft completed the flight without incident, arriving overhead Maison Blanche at around 1100 hrs. Although the airfield had already been taken, it was impossible to tell this from the air, and the pre-arranged ground signal had been forgotten. Telling the pilots by radio whilst en-route that the base was in Allied hands was discounted for security reasons, and it was left to Sqn Ldr Michael Rook to go down for a long, low and slow look around in his Hurricane.

Seeing nothing untoward, he led 'A' Flight in to land and found Edwardes-Jones already there. 'B' Flight flew top cover whilst Rook's flight was refuelled and armed by Servicing Commandos already at Maison Blanche. 'A' Flight then took off to cover 'B' Flight's landing. Meanwhile, three pilots for whom no Hurricanes had been allocated arrived on foot, having come ashore with US troops from a landing craft at East Beach, Algiers. They were Flg Off Trenchard-Smith, Plt Off Snell and Wt Off Caldwell. By all accounts their landing in Africa was just as exciting!

By 0930 hrs the next day Red Section, comprising Sqn Ldr Rook and Flg Off Deuntzer, took off to patrol over Maison Blanche. In the distance, Deuntzer saw two Ju 88s bombing a convoy east of Algiers and chased one of the enemy aircraft off to the north-east, claimed it as damaged. No 43 Sqn's first operational flight in the Mediterranean theatre thus saw the enemy engaged.

Later that day, at around 1630 hrs, the unit was scrambled to deal with enemy aircraft attacking a convoy in Algiers Harbour. Arriving on the scene, No 43 Sqn found a mixed force of He 111s and Ju 88s and went into attack. In the ensuing engagement the following claims were made:

| | |
|---|---|
| Flt Sgt Smith – | one He 111 destroyed |
| Flg Off Barker – | one Ju 88 destroyed ($^1/_3$ share) |
| Flt Sgt Ball – | one Ju 88 destroyed ($^1/_3$ share) |
| Sgt Leeming – | one Ju 88 destroyed ($^1/_3$ share) |
| Sgt Hedderwick – | one Ju 88 damaged |
| Sgt Hermiston – | one Ju 88 damaged |
| Flg Off Trenchard-Smith – | one Ju 88 probably destroyed |
| Flt Lt Lister – | one Ju 88 damaged |

It was a good opening score, although Freddie Lister's Hurricane had been hit in the oil system when he chased his Ju 88 20 miles out to sea, and he was lucky to make it back to Maison Blanche. Here, he found that one of the bombers had slipped through to drop three bombs on No 43 Sqn's new home – albeit that little damage was caused.

At dusk on the 10th 12 enemy aircraft approached from the north-east to attack a convoy in Algiers Harbour. Flg Off 'Paddy' Turkington, on patrol with Sgt Leeming, sighted and attacked a Ju 88 of 1(F)./122. A sharp burst of cannon fire from Turkington sent it flaming onto the beach east of Algiers, the 'kill' being confirmed by Sgt Leeming. The bomber's demise gave the likeable Irishman his opening score in a run of victories that would take him to ace status while serving with No 43 Sqn (his final

Flt Lt Ted Trenchard-Smith busily paints a cartoon fighting cock emblem on his Hurricane's engine cowling panel. Used on many of the squadron aircraft, the emblem depicted a fighting cock with boxing gloves above a black and white check bar

tally with No 43 Sqn, as at 15 December 1943, was five and one shared destroyed and four damaged. He would later claim a further four confirmed and one probable whilst serving with No 241 Sqn).

On the 12th, at 0730 hrs, Sqn Ldr Rook led off a patrol of nine aircraft as escorts for 27 C-47s bound for Bone, where paratroops were dropped on the airfield. All of the squadron aircraft returned to Maison Blanche without incident after an operation which had lasted four hours. At dusk that day a patrol over Bougie encountered enemy aircraft, with three pilots claiming victories. Flg Off Lea destroyed a Do 217 and Flt Lt Lister hit a torpedo-carrying He 111, which exploded. Wg Cdr Pedley (Wing Commander Flying) of No 323 Wing flew with No 43 Sqn on this occasion, claiming a Ju 88 from KG 60 and a He 111 from I./KG26 as both destroyed.

As the pilots landed back safely at Maison Blanche, word reached them that No 43 Sqn's ground party had now docked in Algiers aboard the SS *Strathmore*. This was welcome news indeed for the pilots, who had helped maintain their Hurricanes over the last five days with limited support from RAF Servicing Commandos. Now, the entirety of the squadron was here with its technical support, spares and creature comforts.

No doubt the arrival of the *Strathmore* was equally welcome to those cramped on board, all of whom had endured an uncomfortable and hazardous sea journey to an uncertain destination. Disembarking the next morning, the squadron party marched the long distance to Maison Blanche, arriving hot and weary at around 1600 hrs. As one exhausted airman wryly remarked, 'If I'd wanted to go marching I'd have joined the bloody Army!'

At 1000 hrs on the 13th, Sqn Ldr Rook led six Hurricanes on another escort for C-47s heading to Bone, five aircraft dropping supplies to the US paratroops there.

The next day, Flg Offs Lea and Wills, Wt Off Caldwell and Sgt Hedderwick flew to Djidjelli to carry out operations from there, whilst back at Maison Blanche the Squadron ground parties started unpacking and organising order out of chaos, turning a large Air France hangar into a sort of communal messing facility, sleeping quarters, offices and maintenance section combined.

On the 15th the unit escorted C-47s once again, when 20 aircraft with paratroops headed for Tembessa. Flt Lt Lister led six No 43 Sqn aircraft and six Hurricanes from No 253 Sqn across mountain ranges and through rocky valleys to Tembessa, and although the outward flight was completed without difficulty, bad weather was encountered on the return leg, causing Flg Off Torrance to crash without injury at Djidjelli.

Two days later No 43 Sqn suffered its first casualty in North Africa whilst escorting a cruiser between Algiers and Bougie. Sgt Leadbeatter, flying as No 2 to Wt Off Caldwell, became separated from his leader and did not return. Nothing further was seen or heard of the aeroplane or pilot. That night, at 2130 hrs, Maison Blanche came under attack from enemy aircraft, which bombed and machine gunned the aerodrome and also scattered lethal SD-2 'Butterfly' anti-personnel bombs. No casualties resulted, although the SD-2s remained a hazard for some while.

Convoy patrols were again flown on 19 and 20 November, with a further Dakota escort mission also flown on the 20th. That night, though, was

**Tropicalised Hurricane IIC HV407 FT-S at Maison Blanche, in North Africa, shortly before it was destroyed on 29 November 1942**

**Flt Lt 'Freddie' Lister poses with a No 43 Sqn Hurricane at Maison Blanche in November 1942. The identity of this particular machine remains unknown, but the name *FOO* is noteworthy, as is the artwork – a comic version of the squadron's fighting cock, but in this depiction wearing boxing gloves. The emblem is superimposed above a black and white No 43 Sqn chequerboard stripe, harking back to the halcyon pre-war Fury days!**

marked by a serious attack on Maison Blanche aerodrome by five Ju 88s as the Axis forces woke up to the significance of the place. And well they might. Situated here were three Hurricane and eight Spitfire squadrons, along with a Beaufighter unit. In addition, the USAAF had over 60 C-47s and numerous B-17s, P-38s, P-39s, B-25s and B-26s based at Maison Blanche. In all, an impressive fighting force, and a significant one in terms of the success or otherwise of the North African campaign.

During the air attack that night nine aircraft were destroyed on the ground and another nine damaged, although none from No 43 Sqn. Eleven men were killed and twenty-eight injured, although fortunately no No 43 Sqn personnel were amongst that number. Many of the squadron's tents, though, had been ripped to shreds by bomb splinters.

Patrols at night and day patrols over convoys continued, although one curious entry in the squadron ORB for 23 November states that 'Flg Off Torrance flew to Souk-Ahras on a Secret Mission'. No further light is thrown on what this mission was about.

Until the end of the month the routine patrols continued, although without claim or loss. However, the weather became the enemy during the last week of the month, with torrential rain, wind, and a sea of mud making life at Maison Blanche more than miserable for all. Despite suffering serviceability problems at the end of the month, No 43 Sqn redoubled its efforts in December and completed a record number of patrols and escorts. But despite a total of 1557.30 hours flown during that month – a record for any single-seat fighter squadron – there were no claims. Of equal importance was the fact that again there were no losses either.

Into the New Year, and still at Maison Blanche, 3 January 1943 saw New Zealander Flt Sgt Smith and Sgt Hermiston claim a Ju 88 damaged on a convoy patrol, but on the 6th the enemy returned again to bomb the airfield when a single raider caused damage to three vehicles, three Spitfires and one Hurricane, and also set the petrol dump ablaze. The Hurricane lost was HV561, a No 43 Sqn machine. Flt Sgt Webster, airborne on patrol when the raid began, tried to return to Maison Blanche with engine problems, but had to bale out at Guyotville. Good news on the 6th, though was the award

Air Vice Marshal Sir Arthur Coningham KCB DSO MC DFC AFC (facing the camera with pipe), Gen Carl Spaatz USAAF (Air Officer Commanding North-West Africa) and Air Vice Marshal James Robb CB DSO DFC AFC are seen together at Maison Blanche in December 1942. Behind them is tropicalised Hurricane IIC HV560 FT-Z, which was regularly flown by Sqn Ldr Michael Rook

to Sqn Leader Michael Rook of the DFC for his actions in leading the unit from Gibraltar to Maison Blanche.

The 7th saw an inconclusive interception by Black Section of a Ju 88 that escaped in cloud, the interception taking place over Cap Sigli during a convoy patrol. One week later, the raiders were again back to Maison Blanche, this time killing the squadron's senior medical orderly, Cpl Lewzey, when the Sick Quarters were hit and demolished. He was buried later that day, 14 January, at Il Alia Cemetery.

Still the raids on Maison Blanche continued, with a further strike on the 15th. This time ten aircraft attacked the aerodrome at 1950 hrs. Four airmen were killed and a Spitfire and Hurricane damaged, along with two Beaufighters, an abandoned Air France machine and two Piaggio 100s.

Earlier in the day, Flt Sgt Smith had crashed when taking off for Souk-el-Arba, his Hurricane bursting into flames. He escaped with burns on his face and hands.

The squadron Hurricanes, so grudgingly accepted by the pilots at Gibraltar, had thus far 'done the job', although the pilots were very much aware of their limitations. However, the introduction by the Luftwaffe of high and fast-flying Me 210s caused frustration when squadron pilots found those that they encountered could not be reached. It was therefore with some jubilation that No 43 Sqn heard that it was shortly to be re-equipped with Spitfires.

Despite that, two former American pilots who had served with No 43 Sqn in the UK, John Daniels and John Lewis (who had been unwillingly transferred to the USAAF in September 1942), staged through Maison Blanche in their P-39 Airacobras. What they thought of these aeroplanes is unprintable, and they indicated an eagerness to swap any old beaten-up Hurricane for their P-39s. Their lack of confidence in their machines was not without good reason! To reinforce their point, both men were shot down in Airacobras just a matter of weeks later and made PoWs.

No 43 Sqn's Spitfire love affair began on 14 February, St Valentine's Day, with the delivery of six Mk VCs, and by the 17th of the month all 18 had arrived. After an inconclusive interception on the 15th, the first

A former pilot with No 43 Sqn, American Plt Off John Daniels was subsequently transferred to the USAAF. Posted to North Africa with a P-39 unit, he visited No 43 Sqn at Maison Blanche in his Airacobra, named *RUFUS V*. He was shot down and taken prisoner shortly afterwards

No 43 Sqn's Intelligence Officer, Flt Lt J M 'Spy' Eyles (right), and Flt Lt J J 'Doc' McNair listen as Flg Off R Rayner recounts details of an aerial combat at Jemappes in 1943 (*IWM*)

squadron kill in a Spitfire came on the 22nd, although it was to cost the life of the victor. Eighty miles out to sea in Spitfire ES183, Plt Off 'Slim' Wills hit and crippled a Ju 88. He then radioed 'I've got him. The enemy aircraft is on fire. Going down', then silence. Nothing more was ever heard of the gallant and well liked Canadian. To avenge him, Flt Lts Lister and Reading chased a Ju 88 and claimed it as a 'flamer' as well. It was to be the last victory scored from Maison Blanche.

13 March saw the squadron move to Jemappes, 250 miles east of Algiers, with some of the groundcrews and equipment being ferried by USAAF C-47s and the rest going by road. Although the stay at Jemappes was brief, the tally of victories scored from here was impressive. On the 16th Plt Off Barker claimed yet another Ju 88 and Flg Off Deuntzer's Me 210 had both engines blow up before it crashed into the sea. Another Me 210 attacked by Flg Off Lea was later discovered to have crashed on a beach in Sicily with both crew dead.

On the morning of the 27th, it was the turn of the *Regia Aeronautica* to come in for some attention from the 'Fighting Cocks'. Covering another convoy, Flg Offs Torrance and Turkington shared in the destruction of a solitary Savoia-Marchetti SM.79 torpedo bomber from 105° *Gruppo Aut sil*.

Later that same day, Flg Off Snell and Flt Sgt Hermiston intercepted three more SM.79s, which immediately ditched their torpedoes and made off. Giving chase, Hermiston hit one with cannon and machine gun fire, sending it tumbling into the sea like a falling firebrand. Snell attacked one of the others, and after five bursts it too went down. Turning to the third SM.79, Snell set an engine and wing ablaze before running out of ammunition and leaving Hermiston to finish it off. In a matter of minutes the pair had left three flaming patches of debris on the surface of the sea, all in a straight line and exactly half a mile apart. A few hours later, whilst still

covering the same convoy, Torrance and Turkington drove off two He 111s intent on interfering with the ships in No 43 Sqn's charge.

Into April 1943, and the squadron continued with its round of convoy patrols, but saw no further action before leaving Jemappes for Tingley, further east along the coast, between 16 and 19 April. It was to be a brief stay of little note, except when Flg Off Lea, in partying high spirits, playfully threw a hand-grenade against an outside lavatory. Unfortunately, it was occupied by Freddie Lister (newly promoted to squadron leader), who had also been partying to celebrate his posting to command No 152 Sqn. Lister was peppered with wood splinters, the only consolation being that they were extracted from his rear end by a very pretty American Red

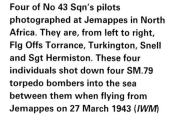

Four of No 43 Sqn's pilots photographed at Jemappes in North Africa. They are, from left to right, Flg Offs Torrance, Turkington, Snell and Sgt Hermiston. These four individuals shot down four SM.79 torpedo bombers into the sea between them when flying from Jemappes on 27 March 1943 (*IWM*)

Staple diet! So disgusted were the airmen of No 43 Sqn with the perpetual diet of bully beef and bread that one of them photographed the main meal of the day in his tin hat. Lloyd Snell, a Canadian groundcrew member with No 43 Sqn, recalled how squadron members supplemented the diet with locally purchased eggs and copious oranges – a luxury, and very rare item, in austere Britain. One day, one of Snell's colleagues received a parcel from home and eagerly tore it open. It contained an orange! Fish, too, were caught in abundance in a particularly productive river until an American unit upstream also began to fish – using hand grenades! Such were the joys of service life (*IWM*)

Cross nurse. 'Besides', said Lister later, 'I could at least brag that I had been wounded on active service!'

From Tingley, on 29 April, No 43 Sqn moved on to Djebel Abiod (thus leaving Algeria for Tunisia) from where the convoy patrols continued. On one such patrol on 12 May Plt Off Richards in JG879 FT-R suffered an engine failure during his pursuit of a Ju 88 and had to ditch, although he was soon rescued by ASR. However, the war in North Africa effectively came to an end around 13 May 1943, but on that same date the squadron was to suffer its last loss of the campaign. Flg Off J P Newton, in JG727 FT-A, ditched while on a convoy patrol after a skirmish with Italian Macchi C.202 fighters operating out of Sardinia. Although he was seen in his dinghy he was not as lucky as Richards for the Walrus sent to find him suffered engine failure. By the time another rescue could be mounted no trace could be found of Newton.

From Djebel Abiod the unit moved on to Mateur, between Bizerta and Tunis, on 26 May, from where it was apparent that No 43 Sqn would be moving out of North Africa in the pending invasion of southern Europe. Once at Mateur, the squadron personnel were told that they were to become part of the Tactical Air Force, and formed immediately into No 324 Wing to await joining up with the other units in the wing (Nos 72, 93, 111 and 243 Sqns) and transitting to the next uncertain destination via Malta.

On 3 June No 43 Sqn moved yet again, to Sfax further up the coast, where it awaited further orders. From here, on 8 June, squadron personnel and equipment embarked on LST 303. On the following day the vessel steamed into Grand Harbour, Valletta, and No 43 Sqn disembarked and headed to Hal Far, where it was joined by the squadron aircraft and pilots on the 11th. Also flying in were the other operational units assigned to No 324 Wing, which was now officially part of the Desert Air Force.

From Hal Far No 43 Sqn flew bomber escort missions to a number of Sicilian targets, and also engaged in three-squadron fighter sweeps to the island. It was during one such sweep on 18 June that New Zealander Flt Sgt M K Brown was shot down off Pozzallo in ES355 FT-S by Feldwebel Reiter of 5./JG 3. Baling out into the sea, he was picked up by the Italians before the Malta-based ASR service could reach the scene.

4 July saw an escort mission to Gerbini for B-25 Mitchells, and although 12 Bf 109s were seen en-route, they turned away and refused to

Sgt J Beedle alongside Spitfire VC BR288 FT-F *ELIZABETH*. Jimmy Beedle served with No 43 Sqn from 1939 through to 1947 as an engine fitter, and post-war was the Secretary of the No 43 Sqn Association, and author of the first squadron history. Continuing to work with aero engines, Beedle found employment post-war as a development engineer with Rolls-Royce

Flt Lt Reading is flanked by his groundcrew, LACs Boyd (left) and Lawrenson, at Jemappes in April 1943. He was subsequently killed in action on 4 July that same year

do battle. Over the target more German fighters intervened, and Flt Lt G J Cox claimed a Bf 109 from JG 53. On the way home Cox and Wt Off P J Hedderwick attacked a train at Vizzini and shot up a blockhouse at Cape Religione. Flt Lt Peter Reading and Flg Off Ron Barker in BR288 FT-F and JK929 FT-A, respectively, failed to return from this sortie, and it is likely that they were shot down by Unteroffizier Wagner of 1./JG 53 and Unteroffizier Grober of 3./JG 53, who both claimed Spitfires destroyed. Reading and Barker were the closest of friends, and it was together that they died.

10 July 1943 saw the invasion of Sicily, with No 43 Sqn providing part of the fighter umbrella over the beaches at first light. Finding a Fw 190, Wt Off Webster sent it spiralling down on fire south of Syracuse, although

Pilots of No 43 Sqn crowd around a recently abandoned Bf 109G of JG 53 'Pik As' at their new airfield on Sicily – probably Comiso (*IWM*)

Sqn Ldr Michael Rook (seated) chats with an unidentified squadron pilot at Jemappes. The date on the blackboard identifies that this photograph was taken on 30 March 1943. At some time during the North African campaign Rook is known to have flown a Hurricane marked with a large white outline of a rook on the rudder. This was possibly FT-Z HV560. Whilst photographic evidence of this marking has been seen by the author, the photo could not be traced for this book (*IWM*)

no other engagements were reported that day by No 43 Sqn. The next day Wt Offs Leeming and Hedderwick claimed a Me 210 which they had pursued at high speed for over 50 miles. On the same day Flg Off Harry Lea suffered a coolant leak in JK616 FT-A and made a forced landing on a mined beach near Pachino, hiding in a fox hole while the battle raged around him. He eventually hitched a ride back to the landing area, and thence journeyed back to Malta via an LST.

Almost as soon as he was back, on the 14th, Lea found himself taking off with the squadron on another patrol which terminated at Comiso airfield, Sicily, which was to be the new operating base of the 'Fighting Cocks'. From here, on 18 July, Plt Off Leeming managed to get his badly shot up Mk V JK612 FT-V back to base, although it was subsequently declared

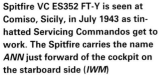

Spitfire VC ES352 FT-Y is seen at Comiso, Sicily, in July 1943 as tin-hatted Servicing Commandos get to work. The Spitfire carries the name *ANN* just forward of the cockpit on the starboard side (*IWM*)

Cat 3 – a write off. He was heard to remark, 'It wouldn't have happened if I'd had a Mk IX'. He may well have been right.

Shortly before No 43 Sqn had left Hal Far, it was joined by a new flight commander, Polish-Russian ace Flt Lt Eugeniusz Horbaczewski, and on 9 August he was promoted to squadron leader and given command of the unit when an exhausted Sqn Ldr Rook was 'rested' with a staff job in Egypt. Each CO brought with him his own style, and 'Horby' was no exception. Aware that the unit had become 'tired', he set to with an almost inexhaustible energy and enthusiasm to turn things around.

In mid August the first six Spitfire IXs arrived on the squadron, and these proved to be most welcome additions to help deal with the Bf 109Gs and Fw 190s that equipped most Axis fighter units. It was notable that No 43 Sqn's combat success with the Mk V in Sicily since the landings was a solitary Bf 109 that had been caught as it took off. In November 1943 the Mk IXs destroyed 14 enemy aircraft in just 65 hours of combat flying. Meanwhile, by contrast, the old Mk Vs still on the squadron had claimed nothing in 175 operational hours.

When No 43 Sqn arrived on Sicily on the 14th it was still partially occupied by Axis forces, and it was not until the 18th that all pockets of resistance had been finally quelled or driven off the island. During this period the unit's primary duty was to help maintain air superiority, with the occasional escort for RAF and USAAF medium bombers carrying out daylight raids on troop concentrations, road junctions or gun positions.

Then, on the 29th, No 43 Sqn moved from the concrete-runwayed Comiso to Panebianco landing ground. Just two hours after its arrival the heavens opened and the landing ground became unusable, resulting in a swift move to Catania Main. From this bomb-cratered airfield, littered with the hulks of over a hundred enemy aeroplanes, the squadron operated for the next two days. On the 31st Plt Off Tony Snell was killed operating from here.

Leading high-altitude cover for a cruiser bombarding mainland Italy in MA572, he was sent after a Ju 88 at 33,000 ft, but was seen to go into a vertical dive from 29,000 ft and crash into the sea. All the signs were that this was a case of anoxia, or oxygen starvation, which had caused Snell to black-out and slump forward over the control column. The loss of experienced fighter pilots like Snell, a veteran of Dieppe, was always a blow to operational fighter squadrons.

At about this time individual aircraft letters seem to have been replaced by numbers, Snell's MA572 being logged as FT-9. No photographic evidence of these markings has yet come to light.

After the brief stay at Catania, it was a case of pack up and move again. This was now a swiftly moving war, with mobility being the key word. Next stop was Cassala, which proved to be the home of No 43 Sqn for a mere four days, during which time its Spitfires flew fighter cover for the invasion now underway through Italy's 'toe'. Pilots encountered and chased several Fw 190s without conclusive result during this period, although it was noteworthy that the presence of the Luftwaffe or *Regia Aeronautica* was, to say the very least, limited.

4 September and the squadron was off again, this time to Falcone on the north coast of Sicily. Squadron personnel now realised that a move to Italy was almost inevitable.

This was the state of the roof of No 43 Sqn's 'new' hangar at Comiso – open to the sky as a result of Allied bombing. Worryingly, a hole in the roof frame marked the entry point of a bomb, and a small patch of disturbed concrete beneath concealed an apparently unexploded weapon. 'Each night', recalled one former No 43 Sqn member, 'we parked any rogue Spitfires over the broken concrete . . . and hoped!'

Flt Sgt T E Johnson of No 43 Sqn, photographed during the North Africa campaign. He claimed a Bf 109 destroyed with the squadron on 22 January 1944 flying Spitfire IX MA400 (*IWM*)

'Benito finito!' The joyful shout rang out across the Falcone vineyards and olive groves where the squadron had encamped, and then rippled across to the dispersed Spitfires nearby. Somebody had heard the American Forces Network broadcast announcing the surrender of the Italians, but it was not over yet. The Italians may have surrendered, but the Germans certainly had not! Clearly, they were still very much a force to be reckoned with in Italy. There was still a long way to go, but on the 9th Allied forces went ashore at Salerno. The 'Fighting Cocks' wondered how long it would be before they followed. They did not have long to wait.

On D+6 an advance ground party from No 43 Sqn were embarked in a LST at Milazzo, headed for the squadron's new base at Tusciano, just south of the Salerno landing area. This was a new landing ground carved out of the Italian countryside in record time by US Army Engineers. Meanwhile, No 43 Sqn and the rest of No 324 Wing (led by Wg Cdr Hugh Dundas DFC) continued its daily round of beachhead patrols, although on 10 September Flt Sgt Leighton suffered engine problems in one of the unit's older Mk VC Spitfires, EF549 FT-E, and ditched alongside a Royal Navy destroyer that plucked him from the sea. Later, he was put ashore. In fact, he actually became the first squadron member to set foot on Italy.

On the 15th, though, there was a better result during one of the now regular beachhead patrols. A pair of Fw 190s were encountered and Sqn Ldr 'Horby' Horbaczewski chased and damaged one of them. The next day things improved when, during a fierce battle with Fw 190s again, 'Horby' shot down two in flames, with a further Fw 190 being claimed by Flt Lt Rayner, the commander of 'B' Flight. Flt Sgt Webster got another, with Flg Off Deuntzer claiming a further Fw 190 damaged.

The advance party was followed out by the squadron's aircraft later on 16 September once the beachhead had been properly established, although in landing at Tusciano (code named Roger landing ground) another of No 43 Sqn's Spitfire VCs was lost when LZ945 FT-W overturned on the bumpy and dusty strip and was written off, without the pilot being hurt. At least the hulk would provide a useful source of hard-to-come-by spares! Following on from Falcone, the rear ground party arrived via the same LST route, but were somewhat disconcerted to come ashore under sporadic shell-fire. It was not what they had anticipated, having been told that the beach landing areas had been properly secured!

No 43 Sqn continued its now established role of beachhead patrols, but this time unhindered by the 90-gallon auxiliary tanks used during the operations over Italy which had been flown from the Sicilian bases. The tanks, whilst essential, were unpopular with both pilots and groundcrew, and also had a marginal ground clearance when taxying and taking-off from rough terrain. The patrols, however, were hampered by attacks on Roger LG by marauding Fw 190s, one of which hit the 'B' Flight dispersal wounding LACs Thompson and Massie.

On 1 October came news, perhaps a little premature, that Naples had fallen, and 'Horby', and the squadron Intelligence Officer, Flt Lt 'Spy' Eyles, set off in a jeep to investigate. One object of the mission was to 'liberate' a working radio in order to be able to listen to the BBC World Service, but the foraging mission got 'Horby' and 'Spy' rather more than they had bargained for! Finding Naples a little less 'liberated' than they had anticipated, the pair found themselves in the city backstreets with their way blocked by a menacing, and very active, Mk VI Tiger tank. Scouting around, 'Horby' located some Sherman tanks of the 7th Armoured Division and directed them back to his Tiger, which was promptly knocked out. Driving back to Roger LG with a hard-won radio set, 'Horby' joked with his Intelligence Officer, asking if he could now be credited with a part share of a Tiger tank kill.

After a spell of torrential rain, with attendant localised flooding that swamped Tusciano, turning it into a mud bath and putting paid, temporarily, to any flying, the squadron finally moved off northwards to Capodichino on 11 October 1943. Inevitably, the name of the airfield was shortened by the British to just 'Cappo'. It would be the unit's home for

Russian-born Pole Sqn Ldr Eugeniusz 'Horby' Horbaczewski came to No 43 Sqn as a flight commander from No 601 Sqn, and was soon promoted to command the squadron in August 1943. He achieved four victories during his time with the squadron, before being posted back to the UK to command No 315 (Polish) Sqn, flying the Mustang III, which is when this photograph was taken. On 18 August 1944 he was shot down and killed over France (*IWM*)

three months, and although the airfield was knocked about there was, instead of mud, nice green turf with newly laid PSP tracking. It was not all good news, though, because on 13 October Sqn Ldr Horbaczewski, 'Horby' to one and all, was posted back to the UK to command Mustang-equipped No 315 (Polish) Sqn. All were just about heartbroken to see him go. His leadership as 'Chief Cock' had been exemplary.

'Horby's' replacement was Flt Lt Peter Parrott DFC (known, of course, as 'Polly'), who was promoted to squadron leader on 16 October, but was then promptly hospitalised with malaria. At about the same time there was a spate of infective hepatitis which decimated the squadron's strength, resulting in pilots and non-flying personnel alike being hospitalised. Parrott was off flying for some while, but the officers who were still fit settled themselves into a requisitioned villa and the remainder of the squadron found a home in the school buildings of nearby Casavatore.

November, and the eventual return of 'Polly' Parrott, saw an up-turn in the squadron's fortunes, with the end of month score standing at 14 enemy aircraft destroyed. All of these had been single-engined fighters, apart from a solitary Ju 88 shot down on the 26th of the month, and of which Sqn Ldr Parrott had claimed a share off Capua in MA481.

The month's hard fighting, though, had resulted in two losses – Wt Off M D Smith, who baled out of JK721 FT-B on the 13th and made a PoW, and Flg Off N H Craig, who disappeared in MA470 FT-8 on the 15th. The wreck of his Spitfire, and his body, was found at map reference G.8495 to the north-west of Mount Maio the following March. It was concluded that he had become lost in cloud whilst on patrol and flown into high ground. The case of Smith was doubly unfortunate in that, tour expired, he had offered to stay on and plug the gaps left by the infective hepatitis scourge. Fate had dealt him an unfortunate hand, but at least he

Sqn Ldr Peter 'Polly' Parrott succeeded Horbaczewski as CO of No 43 Sqn, and he is pictured here outside his tent at Lago, Italy, in February 1944. Parrott, already an ace, increased his score by half a Ju 88 and a Bf 109 damaged during his time with No 43 Sqn

was safe, although it was not until 12 April 1944 that word came through that the New Zealander was in a PoW camp.

As the year drew to a close, a bizarre entry in the Operations Record Book tells how the entire squadron – officers, NCOs and other ranks – was compelled to see a health education film. The content of the film, it is recorded, was so lurid that many of those present fainted, were sick or had to leave the cinema. Suffice to say that the subject matter acted as a sufficient deterrent for the members of No 43 Sqn not to indulge in any liaisons with the ladies of Naples. They, it seemed, were far more dangerous than the Luftwaffe!

The following month was less successful, with a single Bf 109 comprising No 43 Sqn's total bag. Frustratingly, it turned out that enemy air activity in the squadron's patrol areas during this period always seemed to come either just before or after the unit's presence. The pilots joked that the Luftwaffe had heard about No 43 Sqn after the previous month's tally and simply stayed away whenever they were around! In reality, enemy air activity *had* significantly reduced, although this may in part have been attributable to the same problem which now beset No 43 Sqn and the other units of No 324 Wing – the weather.

Again, torrential rain did its worst, playing havoc with operations and morale. The gloom was deepened by the departure early in the new year of squadron stalwarts Rayner, Reid, Smith, Deuntzer, Torrance, Turkington, Webster and Hedderwick. Between them they had amassed an impressive score of kills and, on average, 2000 hours apiece on operations. In itself no mean feat. Turkington, Webster and Hedderwick went back to the Acklington days, and were wholly an integral part of the squadron's life. If any pilots of No 43 Sqn could claim to be fully fledged 'cocks', these were they.

Flt Lt R W Turkington, from Lurgan in Northern Ireland, tells a group of interested No 43 Sqn ground personnel how he shot down a Bf 109 over the Volturno area of Italy on 6 November 1943. This victory took his tally to three kills, and further successes on 10 and 11 November gave him ace status (*IWM*)

# TO ROME

As if to celebrate the New Year, the weather improved enough on 3 January 1944 to allow all the squadron's old Spitfire Vs to be flown out to Bari and exchanged for Mk IXs, thus at last standardising No 43's equipment. Gone were the days of the Mk Vs' flying patrols at a lower altitude, with the remainder of the squadron in the Mk IXs flying 'top cover' above them. Just the day before this change, however, (the 2nd) two of No 43 Sqn's Mk IXs had been lost when Flg Offs Richards (MA627 FT-9) and 'Dickie' Brodie (MA535 FT-8) collided as they came in to land. Brodie was killed in this unfortunate accident.

On the 10th came news that the unit was to move forward to Lago, between Naples and Anzio. Somewhat apprehensively, the squadron adjutant recorded the news in the Operations Record Book thus;

'Told that we shall have to move to Lago in four days' to a weeks' time, and into tents. The weather is now bitterly cold and wet, and the enemy are located 12 miles north of the position we are to occupy.'

It did not sound good, and it wasn't!

Looking in his Italian dictionary, the Intelligence Officer discovered that Lago stood for lake, and when the squadron finally arrived at its new destination on 16 January, that description seemed wholly appropriate. The rain had continued with almost relentless fury, such that dry and dusty weather with its attendant enemy attacks now seemed by far the more preferable. With water and mud everywhere, the conditions could only be described as miserable for all. One joker repainted the squadron badge with a duck in place of the 'Fighting Cock' and posted this new emblem outside the rain-sodden tent that passed as the Flight Office.

A radio mechanic checks the wireless equipment of an unidentified No 43 Sqn Spitfire at Lago, Italy, in February 1944. Noteworthy is the artwork forward of the cockpit, along with the letters *PYFO* (for the benefit of those not educated in slang of the 1940s, 'Pull Your Finger Out!') (*Peter Arnold*)

Under the No 43 Sqn motto *'Gloria Finis'* someone else had chalked 'It will be when it stops bloody raining!' At least the squadron sense of humour apparently remained intact.

Despite the rain and mud, Operation *Shingle* (the Anzio landings) got underway on the 22nd, and during the morning No 43 Sqn flew a 12-aircraft escort for B-25 Mitchells returning from their target. A formation of 20 Bf 109s were encountered and one was destroyed by Plt Off T E Johnson in MA400. The commander of No 324 Wing, Wg Cdr M J Loudon, claimed another Bf 109 as damaged, whilst a Fw 190 was also damaged by Flg Off R W James and two more Focke-Wulf fighters damaged by Flt Lt Laing-Meason. The unit lost Flg Off P J Richards during the engagement, the pilot being posted missing in Spitfire MA589. Later that afternoon an area cover patrol was flown and 14 enemy trucks were left in a damaged condition.

On 5 February more covering patrols over the Anzio beachhead were flown. Returning from the first mission of the day, the squadron shot up a suspected ammunition dump north of Gaeta. Encountering intense flak, Flt Sgt H A Booth, in JG936 FT-C, was hit and managed to limp to the coast, where he baled out near the Dutch gunboat the *Flores*. He was dead, however, by the time the crew pulled him from the water. Australian Wt Off C S Luke, in MH659, was also hit by the wall of anti-aircraft fire and killed. For the remainder of the month the squadron escorted medium bombers striking at a variety of enemy targets as the war moved inexorably northwards. Mostly, these were missions being flown by USAAF and RAF B-25s and B-26s.

On the 17th, during yet another patrol of Anzio, 50+ enemy aircraft were seen, and Sqn Ldr Parrott damaged a Bf 109, although he could not save the inexperienced Flt Sgt J Williams, who had only been with the squadron for seven days. He was shot down and lost in MA576. The month ended with Flt Sgt W A Sutton crashing on take-off on 21 February. Also gone was Wg

As a temporary distraction from the war, Mt Vesuvius erupted with great drama during March 1944, and was photographed here by a No 43 Sqn member. The dust cloud, settling on everything in its path, caused a good deal of harm, and at some airfields down-wind the damage to parked aircraft and material was considerable. Fortunately, No 43 Sqn was not thus affected

Spitfire MJ628 was the aircraft allocated to Wg Cdr du Vivier during his time as commander of No 324 Wing, of which No 43 Sqn was a component unit. It carried his personal markings R-duV

Cdr Dundas DFC, the Officer Commanding the Wing, who had also been posted on. Taking his place was Wg Cdr Malcolm Loudon DFC, whose prior service with No 72 Sqn led him to prefer to fly with that unit on Wing 'Ops'. Not long afterwards he experienced engine failure on a patrol north of Rome, baled out and was captured. Perhaps rather unkindly, the pilots of No 43 Sqn were allegedly heard to murmur that he should have flown with a better squadron! Taking his place, though, was an old No 43 Sqn 'boss', Wg Cdr du Vivier DFC.

There are no prizes, of course, for guessing which squadron *he* preferred to fly with! Perhaps, though, he may have felt he shamed his old squadron when, during a misjudged approach, he made a bad landing and damaged the undercarriage of his personal Spitfire IX MJ628, which, in keeping with most Wing Leaders' aeroplanes, bore his initials R-duV in place of any squadron codes. He need not have worried. Those still on the squadron who remembered du Vivier thought too highly of him to care about such a minor thing as pilot error, and those who did not know him directly knew of him well enough by reputation to know that, despite one ropey landing, here was a fighter pilot *par excellence*.

The last days of April were to herald new rumours of an impending move northwards, but on the 29th Plt Off J P Cunningham was hit by light anti-aircraft fire and his Spitfire (MJ674) was badly damaged. With the elevators unserviceable, the pilot could only achieve horizontal control through manipulation of the tail trim tab only, although he found that control at low speed was ineffective, and thus headed out to sea and ditched, swimming safely ashore.

On 4 May, for yet another Anzio patrol, Wt Off C R Stevenson took off three minutes behind the main formation in MJ483 FT-J and was not seen again. Nothing further was heard from him, and it was assumed that his lone Spitfire was either picked off by hunting Bf 109s or Fw 190s, or fell victim to flak. Equally, his loss could well have been caused by some catastrophic failure or simply by pilot error. Sadly, his was just another name in the long list of Allied pilots who simply flew off never to come back.

Finally, on 19 May, the earlier rumours of a move came to fruition as No 43 Sqn decamped and headed northwards again. This time, the destination was Nettuno, close by to Anzio. From Naples, all the squadron's ground personnel, equipment and stores were transferred to the Anzio beaches by Tank Landing Craft, which made a safe landing not unduly hindered by enemy fire. Meanwhile, the Spitfires were flown into the airfield that had already been utilised by them as a forward emergency strip when operating from Lago, and was thus familiar to the majority of the pilots. The Wing was quite simply following in the train of the advance as the Allies pressed ever more rapidly forward and up the Italian mainland, and so deeper into 'Fortress Europe'.

On the 26th, during an afternoon patrol, Flg Off A W Guest in MJ533 FT-O shot down two Fw 190s as the Luftwaffe again seemed to now be putting in more of an appearance. On the 30th Wt Off R M Carrick in MK118 FT-F claimed one Bf 109 destroyed, its pilot having baled out, and Guest (this time in MJ725 FT-E) claimed another Bf 109 as damaged. The following day was not so good.

During a six-aircraft patrol along the Anzio-Rome line at 17,000 ft, ten bandits were reported in the Lake Bracciano area at 25,000 ft. Climbing to intercept, Flg Off C M Cassels' Spitfire (MJ401) was seen to spin into the lake from 20,000 ft and vanish in a huge sheet of white spray. The No 43 Sqn aircraft had been bounced by Spitfires from another squadron, although it is not clear if they actually opened fire.

Whilst orbiting the place where Cassels had gone in, the three remaining Spitfires (two others had returned earlier to Lago with engine problems) were then jumped by a Bf 109. The Spitfires broke away and one of the pilots managed to get in a short burst but no results were seen. After the break, Red 2, Wt Off J H Saville (in MH509 FT-X), dived away towards the south and called up Red 1 on his radio, saying that he was preparing to land.

Word later came through that Cassels had baled out with slight leg injuries and had been picked up by the Germans and taken to hospital in Rome. Saville had force-landed behind enemy lines with burns, and he too was picked up and taken to the same hospital as Cassels. Later,

Home comforts, Italian style, in 1944, as No 43 Sqn pilots and ground personnel line up for 'tea and a wad' at the squadron NAAFI truck

when the Germans withdrew from Rome, they took Cassels with them, although they left Saville behind in the ward, where he next found himself being looked after by the Royal Army Medical Corps.

On 2 June came orders for a move to Tre-Cancelli, which was completed on 6 June 1944 – a day rather more famous for the Normandy landings than No 43 Sqn's move to another dusty airfield! Tre-Cancelli was an unpleasant and unpopular site, with soft sandy patches causing considerable taxying problems. Here, at this disliked airfield, the unit got to share the same base with its sister squadrons in No 324 Wing for the first time, although the liaison was of but brief duration. Also on the 6th, CO Laing-Meason relinquished his period of command and returned to a posting in the UK – sadly, he was killed not long after in a flying accident in a Tiger Moth at Box Hill in Surrey.

Taking his place was Sqn Ldr A H 'Jeep' Jupp, formerly a flight commander with No 72 Sqn in the same Wing. He was, therefore, well acquainted with all operational aspects of the Wing, knew the tactics and locality, was familiar with the other COs and many of the Wing pilots and also with the problems and difficulties associated with fighting this particular bit of the war. In short, he was readily accepted by those now under his command.

On the 15th, during the next squadron move to Tarquinia, north of Rome, one of the convoys of lorries carrying its personnel detonated a land mine in the village of Civitavecchia, causing serious wounds to LAC Tester, who was removed to the 93rd Evacuation Hospital. Here, he succumbed to his injuries on 18 June. Once settled, though, the squadron upped sticks yet again in the great trek northwards and relocated at Grossetto, 50 miles up country.

Of the unit's time at Grossetto, the Operations Record Book records, 'Little flying. Lots of readiness and stand-by'. It was the same story next month, too. Posted out at this time was Flt Lt 'Dippy' de Pledge, the

**The No 43 Sqn scoreboard, photographed some time during mid 1944. Some 165 kills are shown, although by war's end the 'official' tally of aircraft destroyed by No 43 Sqn was 159**

Sqn Ldr A H 'Jeep' Jupp took over as
Officer Commanding No 43 Sqn in
June 1944, and remained in the post
until March 1945. Here, he briefs
pilots for another sortie from the
south of France

squadron adjutant and keeper of its official diaries since the Acklington days. It was his lot to organise, cajole and seek order amongst No 43 Sqn personnel with each airfield move. In a parody of a rather more famous speech, it was said of de Pledge that, 'Few had ever moved so many airmen so far and with so little transport'. His post was filled by Flt Lt R J Fisher, incoming from No 208 Sqn. Flt Lt Eyles, the Intelligence Officer, was also changed at this time, along with a number of pilots.

So wholesale were the changes that when it came time for the next move, to Piombino, the character of the squadron seemed a whole lot different to that which had arrived at Grossetto. Here it is worthy of mention that, without exception, there was a continual rotation of operational squadron pilots as, indeed, was the case in every RAF flying unit. In the case of groundcrew, in whatever capacity, this was not always the case. A good example is that of James Beedle, who served continuously as a Fitter (Engines) on No 43 Sqn from 1939 to 1947! He was not alone in longevity of squadron service but is a good example. Indeed, his allegiances to the 'Fighting Cocks' continued post-war in his role as Secretary of the No 43 Sqn Association, squadron historian and author of the 1966 squadron history. It is true to say that without his ground work, this particular history would have been that much more difficult to write.

With events in northern Italy now moving towards some sort of conclusion, it was not surprising that, once again, the sojourn of the 'Fighting Cocks' at Piombino was to be but a short one. On 20 July came orders to move on yet again, this time to Calvi, in Corsica. At the end of that month the Operations Record Book stated;

'The month's flying has consisted of sweeps, bomber escorts and patrols. No enemy aircraft have been seen and we have lost no aircraft due to enemy action.'

At Calvi, though, there had been a minor mishap on the 25th when Sgt Morgan made a heavy landing, burst a tyre and caused minor damage to his Spitfire. The next day Flt Sgt Randall crashed on landing at Calvi in MJ577 FT-P.

On 4 August, whilst still flying from Calvi, Flt Lt R V L Griffiths in MH929 FT-Z disappeared in cloud whilst on a sweep. Two days later there was another loss. Early in the afternoon of the 6th 12 Spitfires of No 43 Sqn took off to escort 24 A-20s. Shortly after taking off on this operation Plt Off M F C Simpson crashed in MK118 FT-F and was killed. These Mk IX Spitfires were replaced with Mk VIIIs during the Calvi period, as indeed were the rest of the squadron's Spitfires. The replacement aircraft, with greater range and speed, were better suited to No 43's ongoing role of supporting ground forces by driving and harrying the enemy back across Europe.

20 August saw the unit move 'across the water' to mainland France. Its new home was Ramatuelle, near St Tropez on the fashionable Cote d'Azur, where the major part of the ground party joined up with the rest of the unit, having first been routed back via Naples, and thence on to St Tropez by ship. En-route, Sgt Fackrell was injured in an accident on board ship, and he subsequently died of his injuries. As has been seen throughout this chronicle of events, fatalities and injuries were not exclusively the province of the squadron's pilots.

Five days after arrival at Ramatuelle the unit was off again, this time to Sisteron in the northern Provence region. From here, on 31 August, during an afternoon 'recce' flight Flt Lt A W Guest, in MT680 FT-E, ran into difficulties when his Spitfire caught fire. He had almost made it back home when things literally got too hot and he was forced to bale out, landing safely not far from the camp. Some sources suggest that MT680 was hit by flak, although that version of events is not supported by the official account in the Operations Record Book, which went on to sign the month off with the summary for August 'No enemy aircraft seen. Fifteen motor transport vehicles destroyed and twenty-six damaged'. Those

Spitfire MK118 FT-F shares a corner of Calvi airfield with a USAAF P-51B during July 1944. It was in this aeroplane that Plt Off Simpson was killed when he crashed when landing at Calvi on 6 August 1944 (*via Bruce Robertson*)

All equipped with 90-gallon auxiliary overload tanks, these No 43 Sqn Spitfires were photographed at Ramatuelle, in the south of France, in August 1944 (*IWM*)

Spitfire VIII MT714 FT-F was one of about fifteen Mk VIIIs issued to No 43 Sqn in July 1944. All were then replaced with Mk IXs during October 1944. This shot was taken at Ramatuelle in August 1944, and it illustrates well the primitive conditions under which aircraft had to be worked on. Rain, shine or worse, the work had to continue (*IWM*)

comments reflected the change in direction of No 43 Sqn's prosecution of its particular struggle against the German war machine.

Typical of the squadron's *modus operandi* at this time is its account of the action on 4 September, three days before its departure from Sisteron. The Operations Record Book takes up the story;

'On the second mission of the day the aircraft took off at 1600 hrs and covered the area north of Macon. At Givry they strafed a large truck moving north, our aircraft claiming it as destroyed as a "flamer". Near St Leger another flamer was claimed, this time a 15 cwt type. East of Beaume they shot up a train with the engine in the middle. Hitting the engine, they left it in an excess of steam. The train stopped and the wagons were on fire. A further truck was set on fire and exploded. There was moderate anti-aircraft fire and one Spitfire was hit in the tyre and nosed over on landing, suffering Category 3 damage.'

On the 7th, the 'Fighting Cocks' moved on again, this time to Lyon (Bron), where the locals, somehow, discovered the squadron's motif and enthusiastically welcomed 'Les coqs Anglais!' The very next day it was back to work in the motor transport busting business – an estimated 75 vehicles attacked and set on fire entering Dijon from the south. Then, on the 9th, came a red letter day when No 43 Sqn flew its first sortie over German territory.

Under the hot sun all ranks of No 43 Sqn lend a hand root and stone picking on the newly prepared strip at Ramatuelle. Obviously, such obstructions could be hazardous to the Spitfires operating there (*IWM*)

No 43 Sqn pilots pose with an unidentified Spitfire, probably at Ramatuelle, in the south of France, circa August 1944. Note the USAAF B-25, P-39s and UC-78 Bobcat in the distance (*IWM*)

Led by the No 324 Wing CO, now Wg Cdr Barrie Heath (MJ628), the formation comprised Sqn Ldr Jupp (MT689), Flt Lt Creed (MT664) and Flt Lt Thomas (MT776). Flying a route covering Basle, Mulhousen, Freiburg and Belfort, the formation shot-up trains and strafed motor transport, but encountered no opposition. On another low-level strafe, Flg Off Guest returned with roof tiles lodged in his port radiator housing. Anything that now moved (or didn't move!) on the ground was now fair game, and the sight and sound of Merlin engines across this corner of Europe sent French civilians and retreating Germans alike scurrying for cover. The list of transport-related targets claimed by No 43 Sqn during its period in France is impressive;

51 motor transports destroyed
55 motor transports damaged

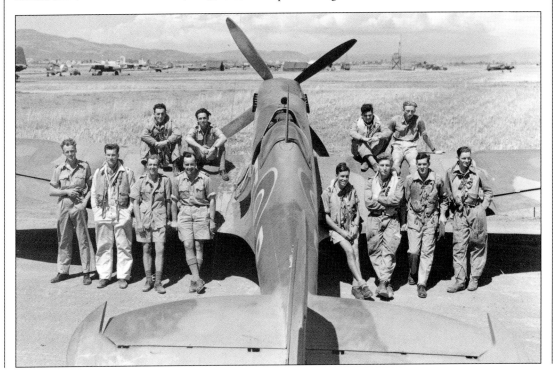

Spitfire MK445 FT-H was the regular mount of Flt Lt 'Happy' Hedderwick, and it is seen at Bron (Lyon), in France, during September 1944 with an underslung 500-lb bomb. This aircraft, flown by Hedderwick, was badly damaged by flak during a dive-bombing attack on 28 December 1944. Hedderwick was later killed in a dive-bombing attack on 8 February 1945

2 locomotives destroyed

3 locomotives damaged

3 railway wagons destroyed

1 tracked howitzer destroyed

2 cyclists killed

120+ horse drawn vehicles damaged

3 horse drawn vehicles destroyed

1 block of buildings storing petrol burned

In addition, almost countless German ground troops must have been killed or wounded in these attacks. It was certainly a terrible harvest that was now being reaped.

On one particular strafing sortie, Flt Lt Browne came upon a marching column of 40 to 50 men. Sweeping down, he watched as his 20 mm cannon and 0.303-in machine guns raked through the German soldiers. There is not any note of triumphalism in his bland comment that his fire 'ploughed right through the column'.

Fighter pilots were used to seeing the anonymous aircraft they attacked fall out of the sky. 'Somehow', said Sqn Ldr 'Jeep' Jupp long after the war, 'that was not personal. We were detached from the human reality. It was just another aeroplane. Now we could almost see the whites of our victims' eyes. We could see them run for cover, or crumple in heaps under our gunfire. We could see their frightened faces as they leapt from burning

As previously mentioned, Spitfire MJ628 was the aircraft allocated to Wg Cdr du Vivier when commanding No 324 Wing. It was duly passed on to his replacement, Wg Cdr Barrie Heath, who had the codes changed to B-H. In this photograph Sqn Ldr Humphreys, CO of No 111 Sqn, walks away from the aircraft with Wg Cdr Heath (*IWM*)

Spitfire MJ755 FT-V is seen at Rimini in December 1944 with its fitter and rigger. This aircraft suffered serious flak damage on 8 September 1944 but survived the war

trucks or ran to escape the hissing and scalding steam of busted locos. We could watch as dozens of terrified horses collapsed in pools of equine blood. It wasn't fun. It was horrible. Grim. Don't let anyone ever tell you otherwise, and don't believe them if they do'.

But now the French adventure was over, and No 43 Sqn's next movement orders sent the unit back to Italy where there was still unfinished business. The arrival back in Italy, on 1 October, at Florence, can only be described as a horrible and bloody nightmare, when a night landing accident turned into a tragedy that threatened the lives of almost half of the squadron's pilots. But it need never have happened. With their Mk VIII Spitfires, No 43 Sqn's pilots had the range to make the transfer flight in one hop, but higher authority had decreed that the entire Wing should land at Bastia for refuelling.

The 'Fighting Cocks' sat and waited as the other Spitfires in the Wing (all Mk IXs and possibly a few old Mk Vs) were fuelled up, although progress was painfully slow. Eventually, it became clear that unless the aircraft got off quickly not everyone would reach Florence in daylight, and No 43 Sqn were ordered off without refuelling. The sensible decision would have been to overnight at Bastia since no operations could commence at Florence until the ground parties were established. Thus, there was no overriding urgency to leave – but then there is a saying about hindsight!

Arriving overhead at Florence in the dusk, No 43 Sqn was ordered to remain in the circuit while the Bastia-refuelled No 111 Sqn was cleared to land. By the time No 43 Sqn was given permission to land it was quite

dark, and so to assist the pilots in what were to be difficult night landings two petrol bowsers were parked to 'illuminate' the runway with their dim blackout headlights. Perhaps, all things considered, the choice of petrol bowsers for this particular task was not exactly wise.

The eleventh aircraft to land, flown by Lt M Duchen of South Africa, struck the cab of one of the tankers with its port wing. Somersaulting, the aircraft came to rest not far beyond the bowser, with the twelfth aircraft already on finals. Flt Lt J L Lowther did not see the wreckage, negotiated the gap between the trucks and smashed headlong at speed into the wreck of Duchen's Spitfire. Immediately, the wreckage burst into flames, and the fire engulfed fuel now trickling from the tanker which Duchen had struck, the resultant explosion spreading to the other tanker as well.

Incredibly, Lowther ran out from the fireball alive but terribly burned around the head and upper body, with just about every scrap of flying clothing burnt off him. Duchen died in the inferno, as did Plt Off Ainslie, a No 111 Sqn pilot who was bravely trying to free him. Lt Dalton, another South African, saw the fire before it had spread into such a conflagration and assumed that a flare had been lit to better aid the landings. Touching down, he too ran into the wreckage, crashed, and was badly hurt around the face and head as he smashed into the reflector gunsight.

With the triple wreckage and blazing fuel now blocking the runway, there was no hope that the five Spitfires still airborne could get down, and they were told to circle and abandon their aircraft once the fuel was exhausted. This must have been a most unsettling instruction to be given, although there seemed to be little alternative. Then, in the true traditions of the US Cavalry (in this case the USAAF), the radio section at Pisa had been listening out to wireless traffic and, hearing of the pilots' dilemma, suggested a divert to their field. Quick calculations indicated that sufficient endurance remained, and led by Flt Sgt 'Wilky' Wilkinson, the remaining five very relieved No 43 Sqn pilots put down at Pisa. Incredibly, two of the Spitfires ran out of fuel as they touched down or taxied in.

Perhaps in part due to the debacle that night, but also the need to re-organise, there was no operational flying from 1 to 16 October.

Spitfire MJ755, formerly of No 43 Sqn, was later transferred to the Royal Hellenic Air Force and is now on public display in Athens – this photograph was taken on 19 September 1992. No 43 Sqn is perhaps unique amongst RAF wartime fighter units in having preserved examples of both a Spitfire and Hurricane that saw action in its colours presently on display (*Peter Arnold*)

Flt Lt Lowther is surrounded by his groundcrew of LACs Ashfield, Hayles, Torrance and Massie at Nettuno (Anzio), Italy, in May 1944. It was in this Spitfire (coded FT-X) that Wt Off Saville was shot down and made a PoW on 13 June 1944. Flt Lt Lowther was badly burned around the head in the landing tragedy at Florence in October 1944

On the 24th, though, six Spitfires were airborne from 0850 to 1010 hrs, having taken off for a sweep over the Verona-Bergamo area. Owing to cloud over Bergamo, the aircraft flew only as far as Brescia. The weather over Bergamo was 10/10ths cloud from 6000 to 14,000 ft, but it was found to be clear over Cremona and further eastwards. Heavy and accurate anti-aircraft fire was experienced from west to south of Bologna, and one aircraft, FT588, flown by Flt Lt I G Thompson was hit. Thompson stayed in his aircraft for a while, but when he saw both ailerons flapping upwards he decided it was time to leave and parachuted out to the south-west of the aerodrome. He walked into the Mess two hours later, the worse only for a few splinters lodged in his thigh.

The month ended with bad weather again, and the pilots, called to a lecture by Flt Lt Perry, Wing Armaments Officer, were astonished to find the subject to be 'Spitfire Bombing'. One wag is said to have commented that 'everyone knows what happens when you bomb a Spitfire! It tends very much to spoil it'. As the lecture got under way it became clear that No 43 Sqn was about to become a dive-bombing outfit. The pilots were stunned.

The Operations Record Book tells how that Perry, rather oddly, likened the bomb and exploder to a fire – coal, wood, paper. 'This' says the ORB 'had a relieving effect upon the pilots'. As they left, so the story goes, (although it might be apocryphal!), another pilot is said to have remarked

The aftermath of the No 43 Sqn Florence landing accident of 1 October 1944. MT786 FT-P was being flown by Lt Duchen of South Africa, who died when his Spitfire struck a petrol bowser in the dark. JF887 FT-U then ran into the wreckage and Flt Lt Lowther was badly burned in the fire which subsequently took hold. Plt Off Ainslie, a No 111 Sqn pilot, was also killed as he tried to rescue Duchen from the wreckage, and another No 43 Sqn pilot, Lt Dalton (South Africa), was also injured when he ran into the wrecked Spitfires. Although there was a serious fire, it was obviously extinguished quite quickly as the Spitfires, although scorched and blackened, are not burnt out (*via Andy Thomas*)

Scrambling for the benefit of the camera, No 43 Sqn pilots run to their waiting Spitfires during the squadron's French journeying

on the coal, wood and paper simile and hit upon a new name for their aircraft – Bomphires! Certainly, it was a name picked up by some elements of the popular press of the period. Could it have originated with No 43 Sqn, perhaps?

11 November brought an unfortunate case of what today would be called 'friendly fire' when the squadron were set upon by six USAAF P-51 Mustangs. Leading six Spitfires from No 43 Sqn on an area cover over Padua, the Wing Leader, Wg Cdr Ernie Wootton DFC, who had taken over No 324 Wing in October, found his aircraft being bounced by the P-51s. Splitting the formation up, he ordered 'Don't shoot!' as it became a case of every man for himself in a game of survival.

Fortunately, the unidentified Mustangs broke off the attack, but not before the Spitfires flown by Flt Lts Creed and Cummings had been badly shot up. Creed had managed to crash-land PV667 on the aerodrome at Rimini (shortly to become the squadron's new home) not badly hurt, but A M Cummings' Spitfire, PT585, was seen to go into a dive and it was later learned that he had been killed. Until a complaint was filed, it appeared that the P-51 pilots had been of the firm conviction that they had intercepted and shot down Bf 109s.

Perforated Steel Planking, or PSP for short, had become a godsend for the mobile air operations that typified the war which now moved across Europe. New runways could literally be rolled out and airfields created wherever they were needed. Such was the case at Rimini, although some No 43 Sqn pilots had cause to curse the PSP as they landed at their new base on 16 November. The PSP set up such a huge rattle when one pilot landed that, it is recorded, he was panicked into believing that his precious beer ration had fallen from its stowage place in the wireless compartment! Another of the Spitfire IXs skidded on the wet planking, slid off and tipped onto its nose in the soft earth. A third had its tailwheel knocked off on the edge of the PSP as it taxied. What happened to any beer ration stowed in the last two fighters is not recorded!

On the 17th the squadron diarist records 'Intensive training began for our dive-bombing future'. For the next five days that was just about all the unit did, and on the 20th it dropped practice smoke bombs to see just how

Defensive high level patrols were flown to cover the invasion of the south of France by No 43 Sqn, and these followed coded patrol lines – dubbed Apples, Pears, Peaches and Grapes on this period squadron map

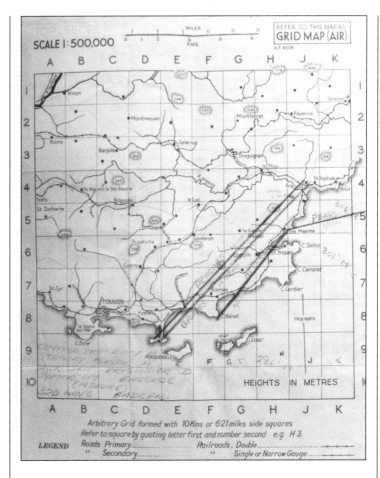

effective was the aim of the pilots. The bombing technique was simple. Pilots were to visually locate the target then dive from 8000 to 4000 ft at at an angle of 60 degrees, with the target visible along the cowling top. At around 4000 ft it was a case of gently pulling out, and when the target had vanished beneath the nose approximately three times the length of the spinner the bomb release tit was pressed. The accepted wisdom was that this would result in odds of three to one against a direct hit.

Sqn Ldr Jupp later recalled this period, telling how that there were sarcastic murmurings amongst some of the more belligerent pilots wanting to know when the squadron was to be transferred to Bomber Command! On 21 November, though, No 43 Sqn flew its first dive-bombing sortie.

The new Wing Leader, South African Lt Col J M Faure DFC, led the first sortie, with No 43's CO, Sqn Ldr Jupp, as his No 2. Six aircraft were allocated to the mission, each armed with a 500-lb bomb, and they attacked a house occupied by the enemy which had become problematical for the Army. It is recorded that all bombs fell in the target area. The weather then took a hand in the fortunes of war and prevented any further operations that month, save for one inconclusive sortie that was flown on the 24th.

Into December 1944, and there was an improvement in the weather. On the 4th, a lovely morning, there continued dive-bombing operations from dawn. During one of these Flt Sgt G R Leigh (PT542) flew through an intense and accurate curtain of flak and was shot down in enemy-held territory and killed.

During many of these dive-bombing sorties Lt Col Faure 'led from the front', frequently flying with No 43 Sqn, and participating with some considerable skill and determination. It is fair to say that he became something of an exponent in the art of dive-bombing with Spitfires, and in March 1945 was awarded the DSO for his work in this sphere of operations.

On 10 December one of the squadron's practice Spitfires crashed on top of an already pranged Kittyhawk, although the pilot was uninjured. It is possible that the pilot was one Flt Lt J P Vickery who, on the 14th, flew a weather reconnaissance flight and returned saying that he 'had seen no weather'. On the 15th he surprised the squadron by turning out in spectacles. The squadron diary goes on to say 'He is off flying and will soon go to Naples to see a specialist. Now we know the secret of his many extra landings!'

With the continuation of dive-bombing sorties, there also continued to be a number of Spitfires returning damaged, shot up by flak to some greater or lesser degree. One of those who did not bring his Spitfire back was New Zealander Flt Lt B H Thomas DFC, when, on 15 December he was hit by intense flak in his bomb dive to the north of Forli. At first it was feared that he had been killed, but he then turned up virtually unscathed some four hours later, having landed his aeroplane, piece by piece, amongst some trees.

Up until Christmas, weather permitting, No 43 Sqn continued to deliver 500-lb bombs to the enemy, although there was respite on Christmas Day when the usual dinners and parties were held with the certain belief that this must surely be the last Christmas of the war. On a tinge of sadness it was noted that, on Boxing Day, the squadron's mascot 'Rissole', a scrawny cockerel acquired from some Italian farmyard, had passed away after a night of over-indulgence. With all due solemnity he was laid to rest, his grave marked with the words 'Rissole. Served No 43 Sqn with no distinction at all. RIP 26 December 1944. Gloria finis?'

Christmas over, and it was back to war for what remained of 1944. On 28 December Flt Lt 'Happy' Hedderwick's Spitfire was badly shot up in the rear fuselage whilst in the bomb dive, and again when pulling out – Hedderwick was now on his second tour with the squadron, having returned as a flight commander.

# THE FINAL SHOW

On New Year's Day 1945 the pace and tempo of combat operations increased with No 43 Sqn flying no less than 12 close support bombing missions. From one of these Plt Off W R Dauphin did not return and was last seen weaving through heavy bursts of 88 mm flak in PV137. On the 3rd, too, there was a loss when Sgt V D Basso, a 19-year-old Rhodesian, went missing over the target area in MK405. His Spitfire was seen to explode in mid-air, other pilots having seen 'spirally white trails moving upwards' just moments before the aircraft was lost. It was assumed that these were some kind of new anti-aircraft rockets.

Basso, despite his age, had become No 43 Sqn's dive-bombing ace, and in 20 attacks he had achieved a 100 per cent success rate. The 4th saw another hot day, with Wt Off C C Hollingsworth's Spitfire shot up in the engine and fuselage during the second mission of the day, although he managed to limp back unhurt into Forli in PT757.

Flt Lt Creed, testing his new Spitfire on 10 January, succeeded in skidding off the PSP tracking and into the mire, only to repeat the episode the very next day. This time the aircraft (PT526 FT-P) was said to have 'collapsed in the mud'. Despite the Category 2 damage, Creed was unhurt, and it was later found that the fighter's tail wheel had been faulty. On the same day, Flt Sgt H Wilkinson led the second show but was hit by flak and injured in the left eye. Sqn Ldr Jupp, Flt Lt I G Thompson and Wt Off A G 'Yogi' Edwards all returned with Category 1 damage from what had been a very hot reception over the target.

Just as the pilots slept in tents and the fitters and riggers carried out their work in the open, the armourers also had to deal with the primitive conditions synonymous with operations on the Italian front. Here, they drag a 500-lb bomb across the ground to a waiting Spitfire prior to the fighter performing yet another dive-bombing attack. Bomb trolleys were not a luxury afforded to this particular theatre of war!

On the 27th a frantic 15 dive-bombing missions were flown, with Flt Lt Creed (PL355) leading the first against a strong-house on the banks of the River Senio. Three bombs were seen to fall up against the wall of the house, and the Army later confirmed that it had been knocked out.

Later, Flt Lt Thompson led a flight against targets on the River Po in PT836, and from this sortie Flt Sgt K F Hindson returned with a 20 mm cannon shell hole in his elevator. Thompson again led six Spitfires off for an armed recce with bombs on 30 January and was badly hit by flak. The reflector gunsight landed in his lap and then fell into the cockpit well, jamming the rudder controls. On landing, his aircraft ran off the runway to the left and slowly nosed up in the soft ground. Flt Lt Creed led a further six aircraft in an attack on barges north of Adria in PT534, but was hit pulling out of his dive. He was heard to call 'Mayday', before calmly stating that he was baling out just north of the Po. It was later learnt that he was a PoW.

The dive-bombing continued, and at the end of January ground attack sorties were being flown deep into Yugoslavia with the dreaded 90-gallon overload tanks. One of these missions had been led by Flt Lt Hedderwick, but on 8 February he was killed when hit by flak in PT712. His aeroplane was seen to turn over and dive straight into the ground three to four miles west of Portmaggione. 'Happy' Hedderwick had flown all of his operational hours with No 43 Sqn – 740 hours in total – from Dieppe to Italy, and was a great loss.

As the war moved so did No 43 Sqn, and on 17 February it was off to Ravenna from where, on the 21st, three more dive-bombing trips were flown. The second was led by Flt Lt King, and over Lake Comachio on the way to the target at 3000 ft, flak was seen bursting two miles off to port. Suddenly, Wt Off M J Mathers (Australian) peeled off to port with brown

**Artwork was not purely the province of the pilots! Here, Sgt 'Spud' Murphy poses by a squadron lorry during a move in Italy in 1945. The bonnet is neatly marked *AL of ORPINGTON***

smoke pouring from his Spitfire, EN296. The brown smoke thickened, turned to white and was followed by a stream of fire. He was seen making for a sand bar, but hit the water just 20 yards short of it and blew up. Mathers was killed.

On 24 February a number of pilots visited Air Ministry Experimental Station 15052 – the euphemistic term used as a cover for radar stations. The purpose of the visit was to discuss plans and tactics for the forthcoming radar control of bombing sorties, the first of which was flown on 2 March in 10/10ths cloud. The results were not seen, and presumably entailed level bombing rather than dive-bombing attacks. By this time, the squadron had also started to drop napalm.

6 March saw the last CO of the war posted in as Sqn Ldr John Hemmingway DFC joined the unit. An experienced fighter pilot, he had served with No 85 Sqn during the now far off Battle of Britain. On this same day, Flt Sgt G D Howarth went missing on a strafing attack, having had to force land inside enemy-held territory five to six miles west of Adria. He reported over the radio that he was 'Okay' after landing, then his aeroplane, PT774 FT-S, was seen to go up in smoke. Fortunately, Howarth was unhurt, but taken prisoner. As Mess Treasurer, his absence caused some grief when it was realised that he still had the mess funds in his battledress pockets!

Although the war was obviously drawing to its close, the dive-bombing continued and the flak was still just as dangerous. On 10 March Wt Off W H Hollis was killed in PL355. Last seen in his bombing dive at around 800 ft, his fighter was seen to catch fire, crash and explode. On the 20th there was another loss when Flt Lt Cecil Manson was shot down by flak in MK549 FT-N. At first it was feared that Manson had been killed, for he was spotted going into a dive from 15,000 ft to attack barges, and was then seen to go into an ever steepening dive until his fighter appeared to crash vertically into the ground. Having only been with the unit for a short while, he eventually returned to No 43 Sqn safe and well on 15 May 1945.

Continuing to pursue the enemy with dive-bombing attacks, No 43 Sqn's Flt Sgt Williams was wounded in the shoulder by small arms fire on

**Flt Sgt Williams of No 43 Sqn was hit in the shoulder by small arms fire in this Spitfire, JL351 FT-F, on 12 April 1945 and did well to get back to Ravenna. JL351 was itself damaged by flak splinters**

Spitfires of No 43 Sqn are seen outside the squadron hangar at Zeltweg, Austria, in early 1946. Note the beeswax sheen on the fighters – such a finish would have been undreamt of just 12 months earlier. Both aircraft have red codes, outlined in white, red spinners with white back plates and black and white tail checks. In the foreground is RK855 FT-C. The serial identity of FT-E cannot be determined

12 April, but did well to get his flak-damaged JL351 back to base. Two days later it was the turn of Wt Off A G Edwards to take hits in RR246 FT-B while strafing a staff car. He was not as lucky and ended up being captured, although his captivity would be short.

On 23 April it was the CO's turn to 'collect a packet' of the infamous German flak. Having destroyed a truck in a bombing attack, he came in again on a strafing run and was at once hit by flak in the tail. His rudder was useless and he pulled away in a climbing turn to 2000 ft, where he was hit again by 20 mm fire. With his cockpit filling with smoke, he turned for friendly territory followed by his No 2. Then, a third hit stopped the engine dead. This is Hemmingway's account of what happened next;

'Before I could even think about an exit, the aircraft was hit yet again in the tail and it pitched violently forward, throwing me out of the cockpit. I landed safely and ran to a farmhouse, but two Germans came after me so I ran off. They chased me for several hours, but I finally lost them by hiding at another farm, where the occupants hid me in a field and fed me with plenty of wine. Eventually, near dusk, I met up with an armoured car of the 27th Lancers and so returned, not much the worse, to Ravenna.'

Hemmingway had been flying PT530, which was coded FT-A. As was often the case, the CO's aeroplane was A, and a new A in the form of MH700 was delivered as a replacement. This particular episode marked the third occasion that Hemmingway had been shot down and forced to bale out, the two previous occasions being during the Battle of Britain.

On the 30 April Sgt A S Crookes became the last No 43 Sqn pilot to be shot down during World War 2 when, in PV193 FT-D, he was hit by flak and forced to crash land four to five miles south-east of Motta. That same day a German delegation were already accepting terms for surrender in Italy at GHQ, Caserta. It was all but over. But there was still time for one last gasp.

Spitfire MA700 FT-A was also photographed at Zeltweg at war's end. By this time, the squadron's black and white checks were re-appearing on the aircraft tails – albeit discreetly

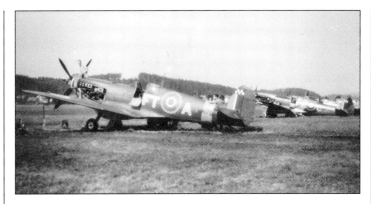

This immediate post-war shot of MH997 FT-J was taken at Klagenfurt, in Austria. In the background stand rows of abandoned Luftwaffe transports. This shot shows to good advantage the red code letter outlined in white and the newly re-applied No 43 Sqn black and white chequer-board markings

Again at Klagenfurt, squadron personnel study voting papers sent from home for the first post-war election. The immaculate finish on the Spitfires is noteworthy – gone is the war weary look. Beeswax polish was applied to give both a sheen and, allegedly, a slight increase in the speed of the Spitfire (*IWM*)

On 1 May, Flt Lts Evans and Armstrong (both of whom had been awarded the DFC on 29 April) led ten squadron aircraft out to attack what were to be the last targets of the war for No 43 Sqn. The rather sad vestiges of a once proud German Army were in headlong and confused retreat. Below, the pilots saw a typical example of this exodus – 40 horse-drawn vehicles, two old motor trucks and a single decker bus all headed northwards. One after the other the ten pilots swept down and raked the doomed column with cannon and machine gun fire. The pilots could not help but reflect on how the tide had turned, and how the Germans just five years ago had chased and harried retreating armies across Europe in just this same way.

On 2 May came the last operational flight of the war by No 43 Sqn. Wt Off K F Hindson in MJ562 and Flt Sgt A A Cooper in PT487 flew off to investigate shipping off Ravenna. The flight was uneventful. Then, it was at last all over.

No 43 Sqn had proudly upheld the historic traditions of what has now become one of the most famous RAF fighter squadrons. In the immediate post-war weeks it moved, with its Spitfires, into Klagenfurt, in Austria. On 10 September the unit moved further north to Zeltweg, and then in 1946 back south to Treviso, in Italy, where it disbanded in May 1947.

Reactivated in February 1949 at its ancestral home of RAF Tangmere, No 43 Sqn has almost ever since been active, and has, over the past five decades, been equipped with Meteors, Hunters, Phantom IIs and now Tornado F 3s. From Tangmere, its bases were Leuchars, Nicosia (Cyprus) and Khormaksar (Aden). Disbanded briefly in 1967, the 'Fighting Cocks' then reformed at Leuchars, in Scotland, on 1 September 1969, and the unit remains here at the time of writing this book.

May No 43 Sqn's fine traditions long continue. *Gloria Finis.*

Possibly the last No 324 Wing Leader's Spitfire (TB539), flown by Wg Cdr T B Beresford and bearing his initials TBB, is seen here with other No 43 Sqn aircraft in a hangar at Zeltweg post-war

Photographic postscript. This formal shot of a newly-reformed No 43 Sqn was taken at Tangmere in 1950 in front of the very same dispersal huts that were occupied by the unit in 1940. Even the black and white chequered flag is flying again! Seated centre is the CO, Sqn Ldr H R 'Dizzy' Allen DFC, who was also a Battle of Britain ace

# APPENDICES

## APPENDIX 1

### OFFICERS COMMANDING No 43 SQN 1937-45

| | | | |
|---|---|---|---|
| Sqn Ldr R E Bain | 2/37 to 11/39 | Sqn Ldr M Rook | 9/42 to 8/43 |
| Sqn Ldr C G Lott | 11/39 to 7/40 | Sqn Ldr E Horbaczewski | 8/43 to 11/43 |
| Sqn Ldr J V C Badger | 7/40 to 8/40 | Sqn Ldr P L Parrott | 11/43 to 3/44 |
| Sqn Ldr C B Hull | 8/40 to 9/40 | Sqn Ldr T B Laing-Meason | 3/44 to 6/44 |
| Sqn Ldr T F D Morgan | 9/40 to 10/41 | Sqn Ldr A H Jupp | 6/44 to 3/45 |
| Sqn Ldr D le Roy du Vivier | 10/41 to 9/42 | Sqn Ldr J A Hemmingway | 3/45 to 12/45 |

## APPENDIX 2

### No 43 SQN BASES

| | | | |
|---|---|---|---|
| Tangmere | 12/26 | Falcone | 6/9/43 |
| Acklington | 18/10/39 | Tusciano | 16/9/43 |
| Wick | 26/2/40 | Capodichino | 11/10/43 |
| Tangmere | 31/5/40 | Lago | 16/1/44 |
| Usworth | 8/9/40 | Nettuno (Anzio) | 19/5/44 |
| Drem | 12/12/40 | Tre-Cancelli | 6/6/44 |
| Acklington | 4/10/41 | Tarquinia | 14/6/44 |
| Tangmere | 16/6/42 | Grossetto | 25/6/44 |
| Kirton-in-Lindsey | 1/9/42 | Piombino | 5/7/44 |
| Maison Blanche | 8/11/42 | Calvi | 20/7/44 |
| Jemappes | 13/3/43 | Ramatuelle | 20/8/44 |
| Tingley | 18/4/43 | Sisteron | 25/8/44 |
| Djebel Abiod | 29/4/43 | Lyon (Bron) | 7/9/44 |
| Mateur | 26/5/43 | La Jasse | 25/9/44 |
| Hal Far | 9/6/43 | Florence | 2/10/44 |
| Comiso | 14/7/43 | Rimini | 16/11/44 |
| Pachino | 1/8/43 | Ravenna | 17/2/45 |
| Panebianco | 27/8/43 | Campoformidio | 5/5/45 |
| Catania | 29/8/43 | Klagenfurt | 11/5/45 |
| Cassala | 31/8/43 | Zeltweg | 10/9/45 |

# APPENDIX 3

## No 43 SQN ROLL OF HONOUR

This Roll of Honour only includes the flying personnel of No 43 Sqn and not the non-flying personnel of the unit who died on active service

18/1/40
Sgt Edwin Gilbert Peter Mullinger. Collided with Sgt Steeley in Hurricane L1734 FT-G at Acklington. He was buried in Chevington Cemetery, Northumberland.

18/1/40
Sgt Henry John Steeley. Collided with the above in Hurricane L2066. He was buried in Kenilworth Cemetery, Warwickshire.

16/4/40
Flg Off Patrick Folkes. Missing in Hurricane N2550 40 miles east south-east of Wick. He is commemorated on Panel 5 of the Runnymede Memorial.

1/6/40
Sgt Terence Arthur Gough. Failed to return from operations over Dunkirk in Hurricane L1758. He is commemorated on Panel 14 of the Runnymede Memorial.

7/6/40
Flg Off John Dudley Edmonds. Shot down over France in Hurricane L1931. He was buried in St Valery-en-Caux Military Cemetery, France.

7/6/40
Flg Off William Campbell Wilkinson. Shot down over France in Hurricane L1847 FT-J. He was buried in Bailleul Neuville Churchyard, France.

15/6/40
Sgt Wilfred Thomas Pratt. Crashed into sea in Hurricane N2615. He was buried in Middlesbrough Cemetery.

19/7/40
Sgt James Alan Buck. Shot down off Selsey by Bf 109s. Baled out of Hurricane P3531 but drowned. He was buried in Stretford Cemetery, Lancashire.

20/7/40
Plt Off Joseph Frederick John Haworth. Shot down by He 115 south of The Needles in Hurricane P3964. He is commemorated on Panel 5 of the Runnymede Memorial.

21/7/40
Plt Off Ricardo Adriani de Mancha. Collided with Bf 109 flown by Leutnant Kroker of 7./JG 27 south of The Needles in Hurricane P3973. Both men killed. Plt Off de Mancha is commemorated on Panel 8 of the Runnymede Memorial.

29/7/40
Plt Off Kenneth Charles Campbell. Killed in forced landing of L1955 near Hawkinge. He was buried in Lympne (St Stephen) Churchyard, Kent.

8/8/40
Plt Off John Cruttenden. Shot down in Hurricane P3781 FT-O south of the Isle of Wight. He is commemorated on Panel 7 of the Runnymede Memorial.

8/8/40
Plt Off Johannes Roelof Stephanus Oelofse. Shot down in Hurricane P3468 south of the Isle of Wight. He was buried in St Andrews Churchyard, Tangmere.

14/8/40
Sgt Herbert Francis Montgomery. Missing in Hurricane L1739 FT-Q during interception south of Beachy Head. He was buried in Senneville-sur-Fecamp Churchyard, France.

30/8/40
Sgt Dennis Noble. Shot down in Hurricane P3179 at Woodhouse Road, Hove. He was buried in East Retford Cemetery, Nottinghamshire.

2/9/40
Plt Off Charles Anthony Woods-Scawen. Shot down near Ivychurch, Kent, in Hurricane V7420. He was buried in Folkestone New Cemetery, Kent.

7/9/40
Flt Lt Caesar Barrand Hull. Shot down in Hurricane V6641 at Purley School, Surrey. He was buried in St Andrews Churchyard, Tangmere.

7/9/40
Flt Lt Richard Carew Reynell. Shot down in Hurricane V7257 at Blackheath, Kent. He was buried in Brookwood Military Cemetery, Surrey.

24/10/40
Sgt Donald Raymond Stoodley. Killed in flying accident in Hurricane V7303 at Usworth. He was buried in Salisbury (London Road) Cemetery, Wiltshire.

27/10/40
Sgt Leonard Vivian Toogood. Killed in flying accident in Hurricane L1963 at Edmondsley. He was buried in Kingston Cemetery, Portsmouth.

4/2/41

Sgt John Richard Stoker. Crashed into sea during air firing practice in Hurricane L1968. He is commemorated on Panel 53 of the Runnymede Memorial.

30/6/41

Sqn Ldr John Vincent Clarence Badger. Shot down in Hurricane V6548 at Woodchurch, Kent, on 30 August 1940 and seriously wounded. Died of his wounds on 30 June 1941. He was buried in St Michaels & All Angels Churchyard, Halton, Buckinghamshire.

1/9/41

Sgt John William Welling. Crashed in River Tay on practice flight in Hurricane IIA Z2520 FT-S. He was buried in Old Windsor Cemetery, Berkshire.

5/9/41

Plt Off David Bourne. Crashed whilst on interception patrol in Hurricane IIA Z2971. He was buried in Dirleton Cemetery, East Lothian.

12/10/41

Sgt John Allan Ryerson Turner. Died in mid-air collision with another No 43 Sqn Hurricane whilst flying Hurricane IIA Z2807 FT-D. He was buried in Chevington Cemetery, Northumberland.

3/11/41

Plt Off Hukum Chand Mehta. Flew into Peel Fell in Hurricane IIA Z3150 FT-V. Cremated at Newcastle Crematorium.

19/11/41

Sgt Robert Denis Bower. Crashed in Hurricane IIA Z2639 on ferry flight. He was buried in Thurlby Churchyard, Lincolnshire.

24/11/41

Sgt Owen Nugent Brady. Crashed in Hurricane IIA Z2772 FT-N on ferry flight. He was buried in Uphall Cemetery, West Lothian.

5/4/42

Flt Sgt Harley Joseph Helbock. Crashed in Hurricane IIB Z2893 FT-L whilst testing the Franks Anti-G suit. He was buried in Chevington Cemetery, Northumberland.

17/4/42

Flt Sgt Alexander John Reed. Killed in low-flying accident in Hurricane IIC Z3068. He was buried in Chevington Cemetery, Northumberland.

20/5/42

Flt Lt Alexander Burnett Hutchison. Crashed when taking off for a Turbinlite patrol in Hurricane IIC BD954 FT-D. He was buried in Aberdeen Springbank Cemetery.

26/7/42

Sgt Ronald Frederick Whitten. Missing from Intruder patrol in Hurricane IIC HL863 FT-T. He was buried in Ste Marie Cemetery, Le Havre, France.

5/8/42

Flt Sgt Alfred George Lynds. Missing from Intruder patrol in Hurricane IIC BN229 FT-D. He was buried in Pont-Audemer Cemetery, Eure, France.

17/11/42

Sgt Leadbeatter (full name not recorded). Missing in Hurricane IIC (no details) on shipping patrol.

22/2/43

Flg Off John Trent Wills. Missing after downing a Ju 88 in Spitfire VC ES183. He is commemorated on the Alamein Memorial.

11/5/43

Sgt Francis Ralph Lane. Crashed on take-off in Spitfire VC JG741 FT-H. He was buried in Bone Cemetery, Annaba, Algeria.

13/5/43

Flg Off John Paul Newton. Ditched on convoy patrol in Spitfire VC after engaging enemy aircraft but not rescued. He was buried in Bone Cemetery, Annaba, Algeria.

4/7/43

Flt Lt Peter William Reading. Missing on sweep in Spitfire VC BR288 FT-F. He is buried in Catania War Cemetery, Sicily.

4/7/43

Flg Off Ronald Owen Barker. Missing on sweep in Spitfire VC JG740 FT-A. He is buried in Catania War Cemetery, Sicily.

31/8/43

Flg Off Anthony Edward Snell. Dived into sea from high altitude in Spitfire IX MA572 FT-9, possibly due to oxygen failure. He is commemorated on the Alamein Memorial.

14/11/43

Flg Off Norman Harold Craig. Missing on patrol in Spitfire IX MA470 FT-8. He was buried in Minturno War Cemetery, Italy.

2/1/44

Plt Off Richard Frederick Charles Brodie. Involved in mid-air collision with another No 43 Sqn Spitfire in MA535 FT-8.

22/1/44

Flg Off P J Richards (full name not recorded). Missing after combat near Anzio in Spitfire IX MA589. He was buried in Rome War Cemetery, Italy.

5/2/44

Flt Sgt Henry Arnold Booth. Shot down by flak in Spitfire IX JG939 FT-C. He is commemorated on the Malta Memorial.

5/2/44

Wt Off C S Luke (full name not recorded). Shot down by flak in Spitfire IX MH659.

17/2/44

Flt Sgt J Williams (full name not recorded). Shot down by enemy fighters(?) in Spitfire IX MA576.

4/5/44

Wt Off Clement Robert Stevenson. Missing en-route to Anzio in Spitfire IX MJ483 FT-J. He is commemorated on the Malta Memorial.

4/8/44

Flt Lt Roland Vivian Langdon Griffiths. Disappeared in cloud during sweep from Calvi in Spitfire MH929 FT-Z. He is commemorated on the Malta Memorial.

6/8/44

Plt Off Maurice Francis Charles Simpson. Crashed on landing at Calvi in Spitfire IX MK118 FT-F. He was buried in Biguglia Cemetery, France (Corsica).

2/10/44

Lt Michael Duchen (SAAF). Killed in multiple landing accident at Florence, possibly in Spitfire IX JF887 FT-L. He was buried in Florence War Cemetery (this cemetery was badly vandalised in April 2001 and it is believed that Duchen's grave was one of these to be desecrated).

11/11/44

Flt Lt Alexander McKay Cummings. Shot down in error by USAAF P-51 Mustangs in Spitfire Mk IX PT585. He was buried in Padua War Cemetery, Italy.

4/12/44

Flt Sgt Geoffrey Robert Leigh. Missing from operational flight in Spitfire IX PT542. He was buried in Forli War Cemetery, Italy.

1/1/45

Plt Off William Ralph Dauphin. Shot down by flak in Spitfire IX PT137 FT-C. He was buried in Faenza War Cemetery, Italy.

3/1/45

Sgt Victor David Basso. Shot down by anti-aircraft rockets in Spitfire IX MK405. He was buried in Faenza War Cemetery, Italy.

11/2/45

Flt Lt Peter John Hedderwick. Spun into ground after flak damage in Spitfire IX PT712 FT-H. He was buried in Faenza War Cemetery, Italy.

21/2/45

Wt Off Michael James Mathers. Shot down by flak in Spitfire IX EN296. He is commemorated on the Malta Memorial.

10/3/45

Wt Off William Henry Holliss. Shot down by flak in Spitfire IX PL355. He was buried in Padua War Cemetery, Italy.

# APPENDIX 4

# No 43 SQN ACES

A considerable number of high-scoring RAF fighter pilots spent time on No 43 Sqn at some time or other during their careers. Some of them did not score any victories at all during their time with the squadron, but later went on to achieve ace status with other units. Some came to No 43 Sqn with claims made on other units, whilst others left the squadron, made claims elsewhere, and then returned to the 'Fighting Cocks' to achieve further victories. This listing includes all pilots who are known to have served on No 43 Sqn and had ace status at the time. It does not include pilots who left No 43 Sqn with either no kills, or insufficient kills at the time of leaving (i.e. less than five) to qualify as an ace. The ranks given are those held by these pilots on leaving No 43 Sqn. The bracketed score is the *final* tally credited to that pilot at the end of the war. Not all of of these claims may necessarily have been achieved whilst serving on the squadron. It is also possible that some aces served on No 43 Sqn but did not score again when with the unit. They have not been included either.

### Sqn Ldr John Vincent Clarence Badger DFC

'Tubby' Badger (8 and 2 shared destroyed, 1 probable and 2 damaged) had served pre-war with No 43 Sqn, and was posted back as a supernumerary squadron leader in July 1940. When Sqn Ldr Lott was shot down and injured on 9 July 1940 he assumed command. All of his kills were claimed on No 43 Sqn. Badger was downed over Kent on 30 August 1940 and impaled on a tree branch when he landed by parachute. He eventually died from his injuries on 30 June 1941. Badger had graduated from RAF Cranwell in 1931 with the Sword of Honour. Mentioned in Despatches and awarded the DFC .

### Plt Off Frank Reginald Carey DFC, DFM

Frank Carey (25 and 3 shared destroyed, 4 unconfirmed destroyed, 3 probables, 1 possible, 8 damaged) started his RAF career as a Metal Rigger AC 1 in 1930 and served with No 43 Sqn at Tangmere. Going on to complete pilot training, he found himself posted back to the unit as a sergeant pilot in 1936. He was commissioned in April 1940. The following month Carey went to No 3 Sqn, where he achieved ace status. He returned to No 43 in July 1940 and was wounded on 18 August after claiming more kills. He became an instructor at No 52 OTU in February 1941, not returning to operational flying until July as CO of No 135 Sqn at Mingaladon, Burma. Carey completed his operational flying in the Far East as Wing Commander leading No 267 Wing. His tally makes him easily the highest scoring No 43 Sqn pilot.

### Flt Lt Graham James Cox DFC

Graham Cox (8 and 3 shared destroyed, 1 probable, 3 and 1 shared damaged) had served in the Battle of Britain with No 152 Sqn, where the majority of his claims had been made. He came to No 43 Sqn as a flight commander in Tunisia during May 1943. On 4 July Cox shot down a Bf 109. This was his only claim with the unit before he moved on to Nos 229 and 92 Sqns. He was awarded a Bar to his DFC in October 1944.

### Sqn Ldr Thomas Frederick Dalton-Morgan DFC

Tom Dalton-Morgan (14 and 3 shared destroyed, 1 probable, 1 damaged) joined No 43 Sqn in June 1940 as commander of 'B' Flight. Shot down with slight wounds on 13 August, he went on to achieve an impressive score, although was again wounded on 6 September. He assumed command of No 43 Sqn on 7 September and on 16 September became Acting Squadron Leader, and CO of the unit. Dalton-Morgan continued to make an increasing number of claims, many of them at night. He left the unit in January 1942, was awarded the DSO the following year and finally went on to command the Ibsley and Middle Wallop Wings.

### Sqn Ldr Daniel Albert Raymond Georges Leroy du Vivier DFC and Bar, C de G (Belge)

'Roy' du Vivier (3 and 2 shared destroyed, 1 and 1 shared probable, 1 damaged) joined No 43 Sqn as a pilot officer in August 1940. Shot down and injured on 2 September, he was posted on recovery to No 229 Sqn. He rejoined No 43 Sqn at the end of the year, where he eventually became a flight commander in 1941 and then, in January 1942, was made CO of the unit. He was the first Belgian to command an RAF unit, and was awarded the DFC and Bar in 1942. Du Vivier was also the first RAF fighter pilot over the Dieppe beachhead. All of his confirmed claims were with No 43 Sqn. He left the unit in September 1942 and scored no more kills. In April 1943 du Vivier led No 324 Wing in the Mediterranean. He died in a motorcycling accident in New York in 1981.

### Plt Off Herbert James Lempriere Hallowes DFM and Bar

Hallowes (17 and 2 shared destroyed, 4 probables, 8 damaged) joined No 43 Sqn as a sergeant pilot in 1936. He commenced his run of claims in February 1940, continuing

through the Battle of France and into the Battle of Britain. Known as 'Hawkeye' due to his exceptional vision, he was also known as 'Uncle' because he often flew aircraft 'U'. Hallowes joined Nos 65 and then 122 Sqns as a flight commander, before becoming CO of No 165 Sqn. In 1944 he led No 504 Sqn, and ended the war as Station Commander of RAF Dunsfold. He was awarded the DFC in June 1943.

### Sqn Ldr Eugeniusz Horbaczewski DFC

'Horby' Horbaczewski (16 and 1 shared destroyed, 1 probable, 1 damaged) was posted to No 43 Sqn as a flight commander in July 1943. He already had eight confirmed and one probable victories. In August 1943 he was appointed CO of No 43 Sqn and led it until October of that year. During his time with 43 Sqn Horbaczewski increased his score by three confirmed and one damaged. He returned to the UK to lead No 315 (Polish) Sqn. Once, he landed in France in his Mustang to pick up a fellow pilot who had been shot down and then successfully flew him back to England. On 18 August 1944 he was shot down and killed over France, claiming his three final victories in that combat. During his RAF service Horbaczewski was awarded the DSO, DFC & Bar, Polish Virtuti Militari 4th & 5th class and Polish Cross of Valour with three bars, but details of the awards and when they were made, are vague.

### Sqn Ldr Caesar Barrand Hull DFC

Caesar Hull (4 and 4 shared destroyed, 1 unconfirmed destroyed, 2 and 1 shared probable, 2 damaged) joined No 43 Sqn in 1936. He saw action with the unit over Scotland in early 1940, but was then posted to No 263 Sqn in Norway, flying Gladiators. On 21 June he was awarded a DFC for his work in Norway. Hull returned to No 43 Sqn as its CO on 31 August but was shot down and killed on 7 September 1940.

### Flt Lt John Ignatius Kilmartin DFC

'Killy' Kilmartin (13 and 2 shared destroyed, 1 damaged) joined No 43 Sqn in late 1937. When war broke out he continued to serve briefly with the unit before being posted to No 1 Sqn in France during November 1939. He returned to No 43 Sqn as a flight commander in August 1940, having achieved all but two of his final score with No 1 Sqn. In April 1941 Kilmartin was posted to command No 602 Sqn, yet despite several other operational tours he had not increased his tally by war's end.

### Sqn Ldr Charles George Lott DFC

George Lott (2 and 3 shared destroyed, 1 unconfirmed destroyed) was posted to command No 43 Sqn in October 1939, and he led the unit in all its early actions over Scotland, Dunkirk and France. On 9 July 1940 he was shot down by a Bf 110 and blinded in one eye, thus ending his operational flying. Lott was awarded a DFC for his command of the unit before 9 July, followed by a DSO in August 1940. He retired from the RAF as an air vice marshal, also with a CB and CBE. Lott achieved the highest rank of any wartime No 43 Sqn pilot, with the highest decorations and awards.

### Flg Off Harold Leslie North
'Knockers' North (1942 DFC citation stated five confirmed kills) joined No 43 Sqn as a pilot officer in November 1939, but his first success did not come until 18 August 1940. Eight days later he was shot down and wounded but returned to the unit in September. He was posted away in December 1940. In 1942 North was with No 457 Sqn, where he claimed a number of his victories. He was lost on a bomber escort to Marquise, France, on 1 May 1942.

### Sgt Peter Ottewill DFM
'Oleo' Ottewill (4 and 2 shared destroyed, 1 unconfirmed destroyed) was a pre-war pilot with No 43 Sqn, and was involved in the early actions over the north of England and Scotland, before taking part in the Battles of Dunkirk and France. His last kill was on 7 June 1940 over France, when he was also shot down and badly burned. Ottewill received the DFM for his actions over France. He did not return to operational flying and retired from the RAF as a group captain, having been awarded a George Medal and an AFC.

### Sqn Ldr Peter Lawrence Parrott DFC
Peter Parrott (5 and 4 shared destroyed, 1 unconfirmed, 1 shared possible, 5 and 2 shared damaged) had served in the Battles of France and Britain with Nos 607, 145 and 605 Sqns, where he obtained the majority of his kills. During his time as CO of No 43 Sqn, Parrott shared a Ju 88 downed off Capua on 26 November 1943 and a Bf 109 damaged on 17 February 1944. Awarded the DFC in October 1940 and a Bar in March 1945, he claimed no further kills after leaving No 43 Sqn.

### Flg Off Wilmer Henry Reid
Wilmer Reid (9 and 1 shared destroyed, 2 damaged, 1 destroyed on ground, 2 probably destroyed on ground) was a Canadian who joined No 43 Sqn in June 1943. He achieved all of claims with this unit over Sicily and Italy. Reid was posted away, tour expired, in January 1944. He saw no further combat, and was awarded the DFC in March 1944.

### Flt Lt John William Charles Simpson DFC
John Simpson (9 and 1 shared destroyed, 1 unconfirmed destroyed, 1 probable, 1 damaged) was another pre-war No 43 Sqn pilot who went on to give distinguished wartime service. He took part in the early battles over the north of the British Isles, then over Dunkirk, France and in the Battle of

Britain, claiming victories throughout. On 19 July 1940 he was shot down and wounded, not returning to the unit until the end of the year. His last claim with No 43 Sqn was a probable Ju 88 over the Tyne on 30 November 1940. Simpson was posted to command No 245 Sqn in Northern Ireland in December 1940, where he claimed his final three victories. Post-war, he held the rank of wing commander but, still serving, he committed suicide on 12 August 1949.

### Flt Lt Peter Wooldridge Townsend DFC
Peter Townsend (9 and 2 shared destroyed, 2 probables, 4 damaged) joined No 43 Sqn in 1937. Posted briefly away, he re-joined the unit and was with it at the start of the war. He was involved in some of the early actions over Scotland and the north-east, where he claimed two and two shared He 111s destroyed. Townsend was awarded a DFC in April 1940, and in May was made CO of No 85 Sqn, where he scored his other kills. He ended the war a wing commander (later group captain), with a DSO and Bar to his DFC.

### Flt Lt Robert Wilkinson Turkington DFC
'Paddy' Turkington (8 and 3 shared destroyed, 1 probable, 4 damaged) joined No 43 Sqn in April 1942 and went with it to North Africa, where he opened his scoring. Between November 1942 and January 1943 he made a number of his claims before going on to No 241 Sqn, where he downed four Bf 109s and one probable. Turkington left this unit in July, posted to command No 601 Sqn, but then returned to command No 241 Sqn in January 1945. He was awarded the DSO in April 1945, but was killed in a flying accident just after VE-Day on 29 July whilst still serving with No 241 Sqn.

### Plt Off Hamilton Charles Upton
Hamilton Upton (10 and 1 shared destroyed, 1 probable) joined No 43 Sqn in February 1940 in time to see early action with the unit, and to participate in the Battles of France and Britain. All of his claims were made with No 43 Sqn between July and September 1940, during which time he was also shot down. Upton left to become a flight commander with No 607 Sqn in September 1940, and received a DFC in April 1941.

### Plt Off Charles Anthony Woods-Scawen DFC
Tony Woods-Scawen (7 destroyed, 1 unconfirmed destroyed, 4 probables, 1 damaged) joined No 43 Sqn in December 1938. He saw much early action, but claimed his first victory over Dunkirk. Known to have very poor eyesight, he more than made up for this with determination and fighting spirit. Shot down four times, Woods-Scawen was finally killed on the fifth occasion when he baled out on 2 September 1940 over Kent. His parachute failed to open and he fell to his death. His DFC was gazetted on 6 September 1940.

# COLOUR PLATES

## 1

**Fury 1 K1928 of Sqn Ldr L H Slatter OC No 43 Sqn Tangmere, May 1931**

Sqn Ldr Slatter was the CO of No 43 Sqn between December 1930 and January 1932. During this period the unit re-equipped with Hawker Furies in May 1931, these replacing the Siskin IIIa aircraft with which the squadron had previously been equipped. Slatter flew K1928 as his personal aircraft for at least part of that period, although he left the squadron in January 1932 and K1928 remained with No 43 Sqn until at August of that same year. During its time with the unit K1928 appeared in variations of the overall silver finish. At one point it had black and white checks and a silver tailfin. At another time it carried a squadron leader's pennant and black and silver checks with a black and white checked fin. This latter marking was thought to have been exclusive to the CO's aeroplane. From No 43 Sqn, this aircraft went to the Home Aircraft Depot, then No 2 Air Servicing Unit, No 5 Flying Training School (FTS) and then No 3 FTS. K1928 was eventually issued to No 1 Air Armament School, where it swung while taxiing and tipped up on its nose at Manby on 28 April 1939. Relegated to the status of an instructional airframe, the aircraft was still in existence on 17 January 1940.

## 2

**Fury I K1939 of Flt Lt John Hawtrey, No 43 Sqn, Tangmere, June 1933**

Again in the overall silver finish with black and white checks, this aircraft sported the fighting cock emblem in a white arrow head, outlined in black, on each side of the tailfin. During this period there is some evidence that flight colours (red or blue) were applied to tailfins and wheel discs to indicate assignment to either 'A' or 'B' Flight. Flt Lt John Hawtrey performed as an aerobatic pilot with No 43 Sqn at the International Air Meeting at Brussels of 11 June 1933 in company with Flg Offs Mermagen and Reynell. This aeroplane was badly damaged when it undershot during a formation landing at Tangmere and hit a boundary fence on 14 September 1937. Classified Beyond Economic Repair, it was Struck off Charge on 8 October 1937.

## 3

**Fury II K8257 of Sgt Frederick Berry, No 43 Sqn, Tangmere, February 1939**

Originally flown in the overall silver finish with black and white checks, this aeroplane, along with all the others on No 43 Sqn, was repainted in camouflage colours at the time of the Munich Crisis. The serial numbers were painted out, although they were faintly visible through the underwing paint of the starboard wing. The port undersides were black and the starboard side white. The uppersurfaces were painted in dark earth and dark green, with wing and fuselage roundels being of the type 'B' version. This Fury II had previously flown with Nos 73 and 87 Sqns, before being transferred to No 43 Sqn, where it was flown by Sgt Berry. In November 1938 No 43 Sqn began to re-equip with the Hurricane I, and K8257 went to the Station Flight at RAF Northolt at the end of February 1939, where it was blown over whilst taxiing on 17 March 1940 and damaged beyond repair. Sgt Berry served with No 43 Sqn from 1936 until going to No 1 Sqn in 1939. He participated in No 43 Sqn's last Fury flight on 2 February 1939, and was killed during the Battle of Britain on 1 September 1940, whilst still with No 1 Sqn. He had been awarded the DFM in August 1940.

## 4

**Hurricane I L1734 of Plt Off John Kilmartin, No 43 Sqn, Tangmere, September 1939**

It was in this aeroplane that Plt Off 'Killy' Kilmartin fired No 43 Sqn's first shots of the war on 8 September 1939, albeit against a loose barrage balloon over Farnborough. It first carried the codes NQ-G, but these became FT-G when the squadron code letters were changed. Kilmartin was posted to No 1 Sqn in November 1939, but later returned to No 43 Sqn in September 1940. L1734 was lost in a mid-air collision at Acklington on 18 January 1940 when flown by Sgt Edwin Mullinger, who was killed. The fighter collided with L2086, flown by Sgt Henry Steeley, who was also killed.

## 5

**Hurricane I L1944 of Flg Off John Edmonds, No 43 Sqn, Acklington, February 1940**

It was in this aeroplane that Flg Off 'Eddy' Edmonds claimed a half share in a He 111 shot down off Acklington on 3 February 1940. Edmonds was later killed in action with No 43 Sqn over France on 7 June 1940 in Hurricane L1931. L1944 was lost in a crash near Hawkinge on 29 July 1940 when being flown by Plt Off Campbell who was killed, although by this time a three-bladed variable pitch de Havilland propeller had been fitted. Other sources incorrectly suggest that this aeroplane was lost in France with No 504 Sqn in May 1940.

## 6

**Hurricane I L1723 of Flg Off Patrick Folkes, No 43 Sqn, Acklington, February 1940**

Also involved in the 3 February 1940 He 111 interception, 'Tiger' Folkes was credited with a half share in L1723. Pre-war, this aeroplane had been coded NQ-N. Flg Off Folkes was killed when N2550 crashed into the North Sea on 16 April 1940. L1723 later went to No 3 Sqn and then No 8 FTS, No 17 Pilots' Advanced Flying Unit and Nos 318 and 183 Sqns, before eventually being finally Struck off Charge (date unknown).

## 7

**Hurricane I L1608 of Sgt Peter Ottewill, No 43 Sqn, Tangmere, June 1940**

Sgt 'Oleo' Ottewill was shot down in flames in this aeroplane over France on 7 June 1940 immediately after having destroyed a Bf 109. Badly burned, he baled out behind enemy lines but was rescued by a French farmer, who smuggled him past the Germans hidden in a hay cart. He spent almost a year in hospital and did not return to operational flying, but was awarded a DFM for his exploits with No 43 Sqn. L1608 had served with Nos 56, 17 and 152 Sqns before being issued to No 43 Sqn.

## 8
### Hurricane I L1592 of Plt Off Anthony Woods-Scawen, No 43 Sqn, Tangmere, June 1940

L1592, although numerically by serial number the first Hurricane on No 43 Sqn's strength, had served with Nos 56, 17 and 87 Sqns prior to being issued to the 'Fighting Cocks'. This aeroplane was fitted with a variable pitch three-bladed propeller and armour plating on 26 May 1940. On 1 June 1940, when being flown by Tony Woods-Scawen over France, it was used to damage a Bf 109, but in return the fighter was also hit, forcing the pilot to make a wheels-up landing back at Tangmere, causing Category 2 damage. Repaired, it eventually found its way to No 615 Sqn, where it suffered more combat damage (this time in the rear fuselage) on 18 August 1940 whilst being flown by Plt Off D J Looker. During its time with No 615 Sqn it was coded KW-Z. This aeroplane was preserved and can now be seen in the Science Museum, London, in its No 615 Sqn markings.

## 9
### Hurricane I L1847 of Sgt James Hallowes, No 43 Sqn, Acklington, February 1940

It was in this aeroplane that No 43 Sqn ace Sgt James Hallowes scored some of his earliest kills. On 3 February 1940 he claimed a He 111 over Whitby and another six days later off Acklington. On 7 June 1940 L1847 was shot down over France and its pilot, Flg Off William 'Wilky' Wilkinson, killed. This aeroplane had served exclusively with No 43 Sqn.

## 10
### Hurricane I P3386 of Sgt Charles Hurry, No 43 Sqn, Tangmere, September 1940

This aeroplane was taken on charge by No 43 Sqn on 19 May 1940 as its first Rotol propeller-fitted Hurricane. It was possibly the single most successful Hurricane on No 43 Sqn during the Battle of Britain, and was never once damaged in action. In the hands of four different pilots it destroyed 12 enemy aircraft during 1940 – Sqn Ldr Lott one Bf 109 destroyed and one damaged on 7 June, Sgt Hallowes two Bf 109s destroyed on 8 August, three Ju 87s destroyed on 16 August and three Ju 87s and one Bf 109 destroyed on 18 August, Plt Off Gorrie a shared kill of a He 111 on 21 July and Sgt Hurry one Bf 109 destroyed on 5 September. Passed to No 1 Ferry Pilot Pool (Unit), the aircraft hit high tension cables in bad weather and overturned at Abbotsley on 16 March 1941 and was written off.

## 11
### Hurricane I P3784 of Sgt James Hallowes, No 43 Sqn, Tangmere, July 1940

Sgt James Hallowes made a wheels up forced landing in this aeroplane at Amberley, West Sussex, on 20 July 1940 after low oil pressure caused engine failure. Hallowes predominantly flew in aircraft coded U, and thus earned the nickname 'Uncle' on No 43 Sqn. Repaired, P3784 went on to serve with Nos 249 and 56 Sqns before going to No 52 OTU and then to the Admiralty in November 1941.

## 12
### Hurricane IIC BN230 of Sqn Ldr Leroy du Vivier, OC No 43 Sqn, Acklington, May 1942

This aeroplane was flown by the CO of No 43 Sqn, Belgian Sqn Ldr Roy du Vivier, during the spring of 1942. On 25 May 1942 he shot down a Ju 88 off Newcastle in company with Plt Off Daniels and Sgt Wik. During this engagement a bullet entered the cockpit of BN230 and passed through du Vivier's Mae West without hitting him, although it inflicted splinter wounds to his face and neck. It was in this same aeroplane that du Vivier led his squadron over Dieppe when flying from Tangmere on 19 August 1942. The fighter featured a personal emblem on both sides of the cockpit, this being crossed RAF and Belgian flags above a No 43 Sqn black and white checked bar.

## 13
### Hurricane IIC BP703 of Plt Off Anthony Snell, No 43 Sqn, Tangmere, August 1942

BP703 was one of a handful of No 43 Sqn Hurricanes painted night black during the summer of 1942 for Intruder operations over France. On 19 August 1942 it was lost on the first of four missions flown that day by No 43 Sqn over Dieppe. Its pilot, Plt Off Tony Snell, baled out and was rescued from the sea, and later returned to the squadron unharmed.

## 14
### Hurricane IIB Z2641 of Sgt J Lewis, No 43 Sqn, Tangmere, August 1942

Whilst little is known of Sgt Lewis, it is known that he flew Z2641 over Dieppe on 19 August 1942. This aeroplane carried the name URUNDI on the port side of the fuselage forward of the cockpit, denoting that it was almost certainly a presentation fighter. The Hurricane provided the backdrop for a series of squadron photographs taken at Tangmere on 20 August 1942 – the day after the Dieppe raid. Z2641 had served with Nos 310 and 132 Sqns before coming to No 43, and then went on to No 245 Sqn and finally No 55 OTU. It was Struck off Charge on 18 June 1945.

## 15
### Hurricane IIC Z5153 of Plt Off Edward Trenchard-Smith, Tangmere, August 1942

This was 'Ted' Trenchard-Smith's usual aeroplane at Tangmere during the summer of 1942, and being an Australian, he had an outline map of the 'mother country' and a kangaroo painted on the port engine cowling. On 19 August 1942, during the first mission over Dieppe, Z5153 was badly damaged in the tail and rear fuselage. Trenchard-Smith managed to nurse the crippled Hurricane back to Tangmere. Once repaired, Z5153 later went to No 245 Sqn, along with most of No 43 Sqn's other Hurricanes, when the unit moved to North Africa. Whilst with No 245 Sqn the aeroplane crashed on 14 November 1942 at Lansdown Hill, west of Charmy Down.

## 16
### Hurricane IIC (tropicalised) HV406 of No 43 Sqn, Gibraltar, November 1942

Flown by an unidentified No 43 Sqn pilot from Gibraltar to Maison Blanche, Algeria, on 8 November 1942, HV406 was one of eighteen war weary Hurricanes selected by squadron pilots from the Gibraltar Aircraft Park. It subsequently served with the unit throughout the North African campaign.

## 17

**Hurricane IIC (tropicalised) HV560 of Sqn Ldr Michael Rook, OC No 43 Sqn, Maison Blanche, December 1942**

It is believed that Sqn Ldr 'Micky' Rook personally flew this Hurricane from Gibraltar to Maison Blanche on 8 November 1942, and thereafter adopted it as 'his' aircraft. Photographs are known to exist of Rook standing by the tail of one of his Hurricanes in North Africa with the port side of the rudder painted with the large white outline of a rook. It is possible that this was HV560.

## 18

**Spitfire VC (tropicalised) BR288 of Flt Lt Peter William Reading, No 43 Sqn, Hal Far, Malta, July 1943**

One of the first Spitfire VCs delivered to No 43 Sqn on 18 February 1943, BR288 became the regular mount of Flt Lt Reading, who was lost on a sweep in this aeroplane on 4 July 1943. The significance of the name *ELIZABETH* on the engine cowling remains unknown. Peter Reading was buried in Catania War Cemetery, Sicily.

## 19

**Spitfire VC (tropicalised) ES352, No 43 Sqn, Pachino, Sicily, August 1943**

No individual pilots or combats have been traced for this No 43 Sqn Spitfire VC, although it served with the unit from 18 February 1943 to August of that year, when it was transferred to No 243 Sqn after an engine change.

## 20

**Spitfire IX MK118 of Plt Off Maurice Simpson, No 43 Sqn, Calvi, Corsica, August 1944**

This Spitfire was flown regularly by Plt Off Simpson of from Piombino, Italy, and then Calvi, Corsica, during the summer of 1944, having been issued to No 43 Sqn in May. Simpson was killed in a landing accident at Calvi in this aeroplane on 6 August 1944.

## 21

**Spitfire IX MH509 of Wt Off J H Saville, No 43 Sqn, Grossetto, Italy, June 1944**

This Spitfire came to No 43 Sqn via the reassembly and distribution point at Casablanca and, in common with most Spitfires routed to squadrons through this centre, the aircraft has its serial number – MH509 – repeated in small stencilled figures over various parts of its skin. This was done in an effort to aid reassembly. The aircraft was flown by most squadron pilots during its time with No 43 from 24 February 1944, including Flt Lt Lowther. On 13 June 1944 it was lost on operations when Wt Off Saville was shot down by a Bf 109 behind enemy lines on the Anzio-Rome patrol line. Making a forced landing, a wounded Saville was quickly made a PoW.

## 22

**Spitfire IX JL351 of Flt Sgt Williams, No 43 Sqn, Ravenna, Italy, April 1945**

JL351 came onto No 43 Sqn strength during November 1944, and was engaged almost exclusively in the dive-bombing and ground attack role. It was during a dive-bombing attack on 12 April 1945 that JL351 was hit by flak and Flt Sgt Williams (his christian name remains unrecorded) was himself wounded in the shoulder by small arms fire. Despite damage to his Spitfire, and painful injuries, Williams managed to fly the aeroplane back to Ravenna. JL351 was sent to No 324 Wing Repair & Service Squadron and finally Struck off Charge on 14 March 1946.

## 23

**Spitfire IX MJ562 of Wt Off K F Hindson, No 43 Sqn, Campoformido, Italy, May 1945**

This Spitfire flew No 43 Sqn's last operational flight of the war on 2 May 1945 in the hands of Wt Off Hindson. The aircraft was sortied to investigate unidentified shipping off Ravenna, but it proved to be an uneventful mission. The aeroplane did not come onto squadron strength until 18 March 1945, and it was flown by Hindson for much of its short time with No 43 Sqn.

## 24

**Spitfire VIII MT776 of Flt Lt B H Thomas, No 43 Sqn, Bron (Lyon), France, September 1944**

The Spitfire IXs of No 43 Sqn were replaced with Mk VIIIs during August 1944, as the latter mark better suited the need for greater range and speed in view of the duties allocated to the unit at this time. MT776 took part in the squadron's first sortie (a transport strafing mission) into Germany on 9 September 1944, flown by New Zealander Flt Lt B H Thomas DFC. When No 43 Sqn re-equipped with Mk IXs again in October 1944, MT776 went to No 417 Sqn. Later, it served with Nos 145 and 92 Sqns, before eventually being Struck off Charge on 14 March 1946.

## 25

**Spitfire VIII MT714 of Flt Lt A W Guest, No 43 Sqn, Ramatuelle, France, August 1944**

One of the fifteen Mk VIIIs that served on No 43 Sqn from August to October 1944, MT714 was flown on occasion by Flt Lt A W Guest, although on 31 August he had to bale out of MT680 FT-E when it caught fire after suffering serious flak damage. This airframe was Struck off Charge on 14 March 1946, although details of its history between October 1944 and March 1946 are vague.

## 26

**Spitfire IX MK445 of Flt Lt Peter Hedderwick, No 43 Sqn, Rimini, Italy, December 1944**

MK445 was regularly flown by Flt Lt 'Happy' Hedderwick (it carried the name *HAPPY* forward of the cockpit on the port side) after its delivery to No 43 Sqn in November 1944. On 28 December the fighter sustained flak damage in the rear fuselage when pulling out from a dive-bombing attack. MK445 was Struck off Charge on 2 August 1945. Hedderwick was killed during another dive-bombing sortie on 8 February 1945. Hit by flak, his Spitfire, PT712, dived into the ground near Portmaggione, Italy.

## 27

**Spitfire IX MK549 of Flt Lt Cecil Manson, No 43 Sqn, Ravenna, Italy, March 1945**

Another of the Spitfire IXs employed by No 43 Sqn, this aircraft also fell victim to flak. With Flt Lt Cecil Manson at the controls on 20 March 1945, the machine was hit by flak and dived vertically into the ground in the region of Fusignano. At first it was feared that Manson had been killed, but he returned safely to the squadron on 15 May 1944. MK549 had previously been used by No 232 Sqn before coming to No 43 Sqn.

## 28
### Spitfire IX MH997 of Lt Armstrong, No 43 Sqn, Campoformido, Italy, May 1945

This aeroplane joined No 43 Sqn on 21 April 1945 and was flown during the last weeks of the war by South African Lt Armstrong (his christian name remains unrecorded). By the time this aeroplane was photographed at Klagenfurt, Austria, in the weeks after VE-Day, it had been adorned with black and white checks on the tailfin. MH997 had previously served previously with the USAAF, then No 1435 Sqn, before coming to No 43 Sqn. It went to No 110 MU on 4 September 1945 and was transferred to the post-war Italian Air Force on 30 May 1946.

## 29
### Spitfire IX MJ628 of Wg Cdr Barrie Heath, OC No 324 Wing, Ramatuelle, France, August 1944

This aeroplane, nominally on the strength of No 43 Sqn from March 1944, was the personal Spitfire of the CO of No 324 Wing during August 1944. It carried both his initials and a wing commander's pennant. MJ628 was Struck off Charge on 18 October 1945 (see also colour plate 30).

## 30
### Spitfire IX MJ628 of Wg Cdr Leroy du Vivier, OC No 324 Wing, Nettuno (Anzio), Italy, May 1944

Spitfire MJ628 had also been the personal mount of Wg Cdr Roy du Vivier during his spell as Wing Leader of No 324 Wing (of which No 43 Sqn was a component unit) in the spring of 1944. It too carried his initials on the fuselage. The aircraft suffered minor damage to its undercarriage during a landing accident when being flown by Wg Cdr du Vivier (see also colour plate 29).

## 31
### Spitfire IX TB539 of Wg Cdr T B Beresford, OC No 324 Wing, Klagenfurt, Austria, Summer 1945

Wg Cdr Beresford was the leader of No 324 Wing post VE-Day, and this was his personal aircraft. It was nominally on the strength of No 43 Sqn from 3 September 1945, and was eventually transferred to the Royal Hellenic Air Force on 27 May 1948 (see also colour plate 32).

## 32
### Spitfire IX TB539 of Wg Cdr Brian Kingcome, OC No 324 Wing, Zeltweg, Austria, Autumn 1945

TB539's codes changed once again when Wg Cdr Beresford was replaced as OC No 324 Wing by Battle of Britain ace Wg Cdr Brian Kingcome. The latter pilot led the wing north to Zeltweg on 10 September 1945 (see also colour plate 31).

## 33
### Spitfire IX LZ949 of No 43 Sqn, Klagenfurt, Austria, June 1945

LZ949 joined No 43 Sqn from No 72 Sqn (another No 324 Wing unit) in February 1945. At this time the Spitfire would have been finished in standard European day fighter camouflage, but on 18 April 1945 it went to No 324 Wing Repair & Servicing Squadron and when returned to No 43 Sqn it had been stripped of its paint, leaving it looking remarkably like a pre-war Fury – the unit colours had thus come full circle. Dubbed the 'Flying Cocoa Tin', LZ949 was passed on to the Italian Air Force on 30 May 1946.

# SELECTED BIBLIOGRAPHY

**Beedle, J** *43(F) Squadron 'The Fighting Cocks'.* Beaumont Aviation Literature, London, 1966

**Bolitho, Hector** *Combat Report.* Batsford, London, 1943

**Cull, Brian** *Spitfires over Sicily.* Grub Street, London, 2000

**Duncan-Smith, W G G** *Spitfire Into Battle.* John Murray, London, 1981

**Franks, Norman** *The Greatest Air Battle.* Grub Street, London, 1992

**Franks, Norman** *Air Battle Dunkirk.* Grub Street, London, 2000

**Lott, C G** *George Lott's Air Force 1922–1959.* unpublished manuscript, circa 1978

**Ramsey, Winston** *Battle of Britain – Then & Now.* Plaistow Press, London, 1980

**Ramsey, Winston G** *Blitz Then & Now.* Plaistow Press, London, 1987

**Saunders, Andy** *RAF Tangmere in Old Photographs.* Sutton Publishing, Stroud, 1992

**Saunders, Andy** *Tangmere Revisited.* Sutton Publishing, Stroud, 1998

**Shores, Chris & Williams, Clive** *Aces High.* Grub Street, London, 1994

**Townsend, Peter** *Duel of Eagles.* Weidenfeld & Nicolson, London, 1970

**Wynn, Kenneth** *Men of The Battle Of Britain.* CCB Publishing, Croydon, 1999

# INDEX

References to illustrations are shown in **bold**. Plates are shown with page and caption locators in brackets.